Bart Giamatti

Bart Giamatti
A PROFILE

ROBERT P. MONCREIFF

YALE UNIVERSITY PRESS

NEW HAVEN & LONDON

Published with assistance from the Louis Stern Memorial Fund.

Various quotations from the speeches and writings of A. Bartlett Giamatti are reprinted with permission from the Estate of Toni S. Giamatti.

Photograph credits: 1, 12, 13, 14, 15, 16, 17: Photographs of Yale-affiliated individuals maintained by the Office of Public Affairs, Yale University (RU 686), Manuscripts and Archives, Yale University Library. 2, 4, 5, 6, 7, 10: Courtesy of Elria Ewing. 3: Mount Holyoke College Archives and Special Collections. 8: Yale Banner. 9: Princeton University Library. 11: Manuscripts and Archives, Yale University Library. 18: David Ottenstein. 19: Brad Trent. 20: Ronald C. Modra/*Sports Illustrated*. 21: Chuck Solomon/*Sports Illustrated*. 22: Michael Marsland/Yale University Office of Public Information.

Designed by James J. Johnson and set in Fairfield Medium types by Keystone Typesetting, Inc. Printed in the United States of America.

Library of Congress Cataloging-in-Publication Data
Moncreiff, Robert P.

Bart Giamatti : a profile / Robert P. Moncreiff.
   p.   cm.
Includes bibliographical references and index.
ISBN: 978-0-300-12187-2 (cloth : alk. paper)
   1. Giamatti, A. Bartlett. 2. Yale University—Presidents—Biography. 3. Baseball commissioners—United States—Biography. I. Title.
LD63301978 .M66 2007
378.1'11—dc22
[B]   2006024009

A catalogue record for this book is available from the British Library.

For Liz

In choosing between ideologues of the Right and of the Left, I choose to reject both because they are finally, in their desire to control and exclude, not different. . . . I offer . . . the view of one not given to extremes but to the middle. My middle view is the view of the centrist, who would, . . . as Alexander Bickel—from whom I have learned much—so eloquently put it, fix "our eyes on that middle distance, where values are provisionally held, are tested, and evolve— derived from the morality of process, which is the morality of consent."

—A. BARTLETT GIAMATTI, in his baccalaureate address to the senior class in Yale College, May 1982.

ALEXANDER BICKEL was a professor at the Yale Law School from 1956 until his death in 1974 at the age of forty-nine.

Contents

Yale: University President

Baseball

Illustrations follow page 82

Preface

I never knew Bart Giamatti. We had similar experiences as Yale undergraduates, belonging to several of the same organizations and pursuing the same intensive major in English, but I graduated eight years before he did. And when my education veered away from graduate training for an academic career and into the law, there was no occasion for our paths to cross. As an alumnus with a continuing interest in English literature, I was distantly aware of him as a rising star in the Yale English department. I always admired him from afar, but it was not until my son entered Yale as an undergraduate in 1976 and Giamatti became president of the university two years later that my admiration became focused and intensified. I followed his career more closely after that (though still from afar), through the tribulations of his later years as Yale's president and the drama of his confrontation with Pete Rose until his startling early death in 1989.

Retired professional persons—I became one at age sixty-five after a career as a corporate lawyer in a large metropolitan law firm—need projects with some intellectual content, and it occurred to me one day to look into whether anything had been

written for publication about Bart Giamatti. It turned out that
there wasn't much. The best book about him, *Collision at
Home Plate*, which the author, James Reston, Jr., characterizes
as a "dual biography" of Giamatti and Pete Rose, is very good
on Giamatti, but understandably weighted toward his brief
service as a baseball executive. There was clearly room for a
more balanced study. I asked Yale Emeritus Sterling Professor
of English Literature Maynard Mack, a teacher of mine and a
mentor of Giamatti's, whether he knew of anything I had
missed or any work in progress. He didn't. Full steam ahead, he
said, you'll have some fun.

It *was* fun to find validation in Giamatti's life and writing
for all I admired that had led me to undertake the project in the
first place. There was Giamatti's eloquence and wit. His brilliant teaching. His imaginative scholarship, rooted in the late
Middle Ages and the Renaissance, whose model of the cosmos
was what Giamatti's poet Edmund Spenser called "the principle of Order and Permanence which created the world, and . . .
remains always above it," giving coherence to everything below, where mutability and chance reign and threaten chaos.
There was his respect and love for baseball, exemplifying for
him the importance of order imposed on activity that would
otherwise be random; and for the Boston Red Sox in particular,
whose history carries for its fans, Giamatti among them, the
heartbreak of living in an uncertain world. And above all, arising out of the rest, there was his role as a defender of tradition,
of order, moderation, and restraint in all things—in literature,
in educational philosophy and standards, in political conduct,
a role made more vivid because lived out against the background of a culture in which such values were under attack
and widely out of favor.

But there was a dark side to Giamatti's personality, an insecurity manifested by acute sensitivity to criticism and frus-

trated idealism, that caused him great personal anguish and sometimes limited his effectiveness. Some of his colleagues and others saw his personal vulnerability as the source of weaknesses that caused him to fail as Yale's president. Nearly everyone acknowledged that it clouded his life and contributed to its premature end. A senior participant in Yale affairs during the Giamatti years, who described her association with him as among the richest experiences of her career, summarized it thus: "I don't think he was a very happy man."

The source of this insecurity is obscure. He grew up in a happy and loving family environment, among boyhood companions who knew he was smart but thought he was otherwise just like them. He was high-strung and a worrier as a child, but as a student, teacher, and scholar thereafter he moved from one success to another, liked, admired, and respected by friends, students, and colleagues through a near-meteoric academic career. But as early as his college years we begin to see an exaggerated need for recognition and approval. He was ambitious for positions of leadership. He badly wanted acceptance by the world around him, but the very wit and charisma that drew people to him—the scintillating actor's persona he invented to define himself—developed into a shield and a defense against the outside world. When he grew older, his family became, in the best Italian tradition, a private refuge, a place, as he once wrote, "where one does not have to be on guard, where one can assume support and nurture."

Disorder is the enemy of insecurity. The confident person half expects it, minimizes it, rises above it; there is no matter of principle involved in the breakdown of order. Such a person is praised as being flexible, adaptive, as having a "thick skin." Not so Giamatti. In his ideal world, order meant more than a desired state of affairs created by the absence of discord (though that is a predominant meaning in many of his speeches). It was the right arrangement of relationships between persons and their respective responsibilities that makes possible freedom to engage in constructive activity. As he said over and over again in a variety of places and ways: "A civilized order is the precondition of freedom, and freedom the goal of responsible order." Order is the keystone in an ideal arch that collapses when order fails.

The genesis of Giamatti's idealization of order as the indispensable condition for human achievement is not readily apparent. Perhaps it was natural in a boy raised in a family presided over by a traditional Italian father steeped in the ordered world of Dante. It may have been a defense raised by Giamatti himself against his insecurities. He certainly found reinforcement for it in his literary models, from Dante through Spenser to the greatest of Renaissance poets, Shakespeare: "Take but degree away," says Ulysses in his famous apostrophe to order in *Troilus and Cressida,* "untune that string, / And hark what discord follows." Whatever its source, it was a powerful force in Giamatti's life.

Critics of Giamatti as president of Yale believed that his ideal world of order and freedom did not provide a sound basis for confronting and managing the complexities of the modern multiversity. But the damage came not from the inadequacy of the ideal but from the terrible personal toll exacted on the vulnerable Giamatti when it proved unattainable.

In the affair that defined Giamatti's career as a baseball executive—the conflict with Pete Rose over Rose's betting on baseball games—the inevitable delays and uncertainties of the judicial process, and the attendant carping of the media, created the disorder and caused the personal anguish. Fortunately, in that case the disorder resolved itself, though it left Giamatti exhausted, and he was able to put an end to the affair with a public statement that vindicated his ideals for the game.

Competing assessments of Giamatti's success and importance as a university president are set forth in what follows,
and readers will reach their own conclusions. But I hope every
reader will come to agree with the sentiment expressed in an
unsolicited letter to the author from a high school classmate of
long ago, the wife of a Yale alumnus, writing because she recognized my name in a request in her husband's copy of the *Yale
Alumni Magazine* for recollections by students. She never
knew Giamatti personally, she wrote, but "I always thought he
was the most interesting Yale president in modern times."

The title of this book calls it a "profile" rather than a "life"
or a "biography." The term is intended to reflect certain limitations on the sources available to the author that need to be
noted, not to complain or extenuate, but as a guide for measuring completeness.

The first of these was imposed by Yale University, which has a
policy of denying access to the official papers of presidents and
other major officers and administrators for thirty-five years from
the date when the person leaves office; in Giamatti's case the files
are sealed until 2021. I thus have not seen Giamatti's presidential
papers, nor those of any member of his administration.

The second limitation was the unwillingness of Giamatti's
widow, and therefore quite understandably his children, to talk
to me or to make available any papers and other materials in
their possession. Toni Giamatti, never comfortable in public,
became, say many who knew her (she died in 2004), increasingly reclusive after her husband's death. Her silence closed
off access to Giamatti's home life. I have resisted the temptation to speculate on what I cannot know.

It should be recorded, however, that Giamatti's mother and
his siblings, particularly his sister Elria Ewing, were graciously
cooperative in telling me about Bart's family and helping me to

understand his early years in South Hadley, Massachusetts. Thanks are also due to Giamatti's children for their kind willingness to permit the use in the book of quotations from his speeches and writings.

These limitations have, of course, been disappointing. It is considerable consolation to reflect, however, that my work has had the benefit of the recollections and judgments of many people that may not be available to a biographer writing when (or, in the case of individuals, if) the limitations cease to be operative.

Acknowledgments

Countless people contributed to this book, but a few deserve special thanks:

First and last, my peerless wife, initial reader of every chapter, with a keen eye for clumsy syntax and dubious judgments, but above all the unfailing source of encouragement through all the writing and waiting. This book is dedicated to her.

The late Maynard Mack, who, when his initial noncommittal encouragement to a former student ("you'll have some fun") developed into genuine enthusiasm for the project, urged me to write the book and advocated effectively for its publication.

John Wilkinson, Giamatti's close friend, a central figure in his administration and that of Kingman Brewster before him, whose sound judgment in all Yale matters and wide contacts throughout the university were invaluable.

The staff of the Manuscript and Archives section of the Yale Sterling Memorial Library, especially Bill Massa, the encyclopedic public service archivist, and, if I may be permitted to single out two others for their special help, Sandra Staton and Michael Frost.

The library staff of my own law firm of Edwards Angell

Palmer & Dodge LLP, especially research librarian Joe Pollender, for countless searches and finds.

Elaine Spinale, secretary and friend, competent, cheerful and patient, whose many indispensable services included extricating the author when the complexities of the modern computer, unknown in his years of active law practice, threatened to overwhelm him.

An alphabetical list of the many persons who spoke to me about Giamatti is included at the end of the section on Notes and Sources. All provided valuable help. Some of those on whose insights I drew most heavily are named and credited elsewhere in the notes.

I want finally to thank two old friends who advised at various stages during the preparation of the manuscript: my colleague at Edwards Angell Palmer & Dodge, Peter Terris, and Christopher Reed, executive editor of *Harvard Magazine*.

Beginnings

Boyhood

Angelo Bartlett Giamatti—Bart to everyone—was born in Boston, Massachusetts, on April 4, 1938. He was named for his two grandfathers, Angelo Giamatti on his father's side and Bartlett Walton on his mother's. Angelo was an Italian immigrant from a small village near Naples. He settled in New Haven, Connecticut, where his son Valentine, Bart's father, was born and raised. Bartlett Walton, whose daughter Mary—always called Peggy—was Bart's mother, raised his family in Wakefield, Massachusetts, a suburb of Boston. Angelo Giamatti was a laborer at the New Haven Clock Company, and the family—there were five children, four girls and a boy—lived in modest, even straitened, circumstances on Lilac Street in New Haven, then an enclave of Italian immigrants. The Waltons, by contrast, lived in relative affluence in Wakefield, for Bartlett Walton's father was the founder of a successful shoe manufacturing concern, and there was a substantial inheritance for Bartlett, his wife, and three daughters.

Valentine Giamatti—Val—attended Hillhouse High School in New Haven, then located near the heart of the Yale University campus. He excelled academically and earned admission to Yale as a day student on one of the Sterling Memorial Scholarships, for which preference was given to New Haven high school graduates. His academic success continued at the university, and when he graduated as a member of Phi Beta Kappa in 1932, he qualified for a fellowship that permitted him to become a graduate student at Yale in the field of Romance languages. At the beginning of the subsequent academic year of 1933–34 he sailed to Italy to continue his studies under an exchange fellowship at the University of Florence. On shipboard he met Peggy Walton, handsome, charming, and smart, traveling to spend her junior year at Smith College abroad in the study of Italian language and literature. There began a courtship that continued through Peggy's senior year at Smith and a year beyond, while Val was back at Yale continuing graduate work. The culture shock of introducing Peggy to Val's immigrant parents and him to her Yankee family was successfully overcome, and in July 1936 Valentine Giamatti and Peggy Walton were married.

Giamatti had reached an impasse with Yale over the choice of a subject for his dissertation—exacerbated, perhaps, by doubts of a conservative faculty member as to the academic commitment of a man who had decided to marry and begin a family before completing his Ph.D.—and he did not return to New Haven. Instead he accepted an offer to teach Romance languages at the newly established Vermont Junior College, and the Giamattis spent the first three years of their married life in Montpelier. It was during this period that Bart was born.

Valentine Giamatti knew that he needed a Ph.D. to progress in the academic profession. On the suggestion of a colleague he applied to Harvard, which agreed to accept all of his Yale course credits. Harvard also approved the dissertation subject that Yale had rejected, an account of the service in the American Revolution of one Chevalier Luigi Antonio Cambray

Digny, a Frenchman born of a Florentine family, based on an archive made available to Giamatti during his year in Florence. So the academic year 1939–40 was spent in Cambridge, Massachusetts, at the end of which he had earned a Ph.D. in Romance languages.

In the spring of that year the phone rang in the Giamatti apartment in Cambridge, and a stranger, the head of the French department at Mount Holyoke, the distinguished women's college in South Hadley, Massachusetts, inquired whether the young Harvard Ph.D.-to-be would be interested in joining the faculty as an instructor in Italian language and literature. Giamatti had to ask his wife where South Hadley was, but it was a splendid and wholly unexpected opportunity. So the family, which now included a baby daughter Elena Maria—always Elria after her brother Bart had so dubbed her —moved in 1940 to the small New England college town on the Connecticut River in western Massachusetts, and Valentine Giamatti began the career which was to extend without interruption until his retirement in 1973. After a couple of years in rented quarters, the Giamatti family bought a comfortable Colonial house on a corner lot on Silver Street north of the campus, with a fine view over its playing fields down to the cluster of weathered nineteenth-century red brick buildings along College Street that define the college. A second son, Dino, was born in 1943.

Giamatti was a commanding presence throughout his teaching career at Mount Holyoke. The warmth of his outgoing personality and his capacity for friendship attracted the young women of the college: he was the marvelous Mr. G., and they flocked to him. His lecture course on "Dante and His Times," conducted in English, was a rite of passage for those who were not students of the Italian language, and for those who were, there were the seminars on Dante in Italian, which met in his living room on Silver Street. For several years in the late 1940s and early 1950s he and his students organized a so-called Dante Fair in the spring on the large lot behind his house to benefit a home for poor and wayward boys north of Rome. Students marched from the center of town behind a fire truck, and people came from miles around to participate in a program of games and other attractions, including fortune-tellers, a spike-driving contest, turtle races, and horses for children's rides.

Giamatti's activities were not limited to the campus. He was a familiar figure throughout South Hadley, talking informally with townspeople wherever he found them, and serving at various times as a representative to the town meeting and as a P.T.A. president. He was a popular public speaker to groups of Mount Holyoke alumnae and others. Whatever indignities of prejudice he had suffered as a child of Italian immigrants in New Haven, and there must have been many, had been left behind, overcome by his fundamentally sunny spirit in the liberating freshness of a small New England college town and his pride in the literature and culture of Italy that were at the center of his intellectual life.

He was a teacher first and foremost. His published output was slim: an introductory Italian grammar that arose out of his teaching of the Italian language at Mount Holyoke; a visual rendering of the schematics of Dante's *Divine Comedy* entitled "Panoramic Views of Dante's Inferno, Purgatory and Paradise"; a few translations. His family believes that the small quantity of written scholarship reflected a kind of writer's block in English, which he had begun to learn only when he was a young second-generation immigrant schoolboy in New Haven. Whatever the reason, his intellectual curiosity expressed itself in other ways. He was an ardent collector: of illustrated editions of the *Divine Comedy* going back to the fifteenth century—his collection of more than 140 volumes in twenty-one languages, now in the Mount Holyoke College Library, is one of the world's finest; of Etruscan pottery; of Roman coins. The Giamattis built an addition to their house on Silver Street in the 1950s to maintain these collections in climate-controlled conditions. As his collections reveal, any small interest became an enormous interest, pursued with an all-embracing enthusiasm.

His family adored him. To them he was Babbo—Daddy. When he retired from the faculty in 1973, his family and friends organized a great party, attended by more than a hundred people and extending over a weekend, at the hotel on the Maine seacoast then owned by his younger son Dino. His retirement present was a gray granite bench inscribed with an English translation of lines from Dante's *Divine Comedy*. They come in the second section of the poem, *Purgatory*, where Dante's guide, Virgil, is explaining that when the sinner has been purged of the sin of envy, he is free to seek in fellowship with others those things which, enriching each, at the same time enrich everyone, so that the more that are enriched, the richer is each. Love is such a thing. This is the inscription: "The more on earth there are of loving hearts the more worth loving, and the more the love, which, like a mirror, each to each imparts." Babbo's Bench was originally placed on the lawn of Dino Giamatti's hotel, facing the sea. When the hotel was sold in 1987, the bench was moved to a small plot on the campus of Mount Holyoke, just outside Valentine Giamatti's old office, where it still stands.

Peggy Giamatti was fully her husband's partner in the life of the family. From her came, her son Dino remembers, "our value system, the way we were brought up." Her husband, far from his New Haven roots, adopted as his own the New England identity and lifestyle of his wife. She contributed, too, an important dimension to the family's cultural life. She was an accomplished pianist; the children's love of opera began with her. She made herself a sophisticated amateur art historian; it was she who organized and led the visits to the treasures of Italy when the family was on sabbatical. Fluent in its language, her knowledge of and devotion to the culture of Italy complemented and enriched that of her husband.

This loving and richly intellectual environment was the world of Bart Giamatti's boyhood. He was a high-spirited and mischievous boy, the ringleader among his best friends Billy Mazeine, Andy Vitali, and Frankie White. There were pranks—his sister Elria remembers the occasion when the boys, posing as itinerant salesmen of Christmas decorations, sold to a distinguished faculty member, the poet Peter Viereck, the wreath that they had stolen from his front door only moments before. There were trips to the movies in nearby Holyoke, sometimes in the high school years with dates, followed by something to eat at Friendly's restaurant. Bart was the entertainer, the actor, on stage with his impersonations, the zany comedian Jerry Lewis and sob singer Johnnie Ray among them. There were periods, especially on weekends, of simply hanging out at the various houses of the boys, or more often, at Hector's pool hall on College Street, where a game of pool was a nickel and the boys learned to smoke. And there were sports, especially baseball, in which Bart did not excel—he was never more than an indifferent athlete—but in which he was intensely interested, finding vicarious participation as manager of the high school baseball team. Long before he became an executive in organized baseball, it occupied a special place in Giamatti's life, for he saw mirrored in it the ordered striving he sought in all things. He saw also in it, ruefully, the inevitability of disappointment inherent in the game's uncertainties.

The Boston Red Sox Giamatti learned to love as a small boy

in the 1940s were in the early stages of living out the consequences, operative until they finally won a World Series in 2004,
of "The Curse of the Bambino." As explained by *Boston Globe*
sportswriter Dan Shaughnessy in a book by that name, this was
a spell that the Red Sox placed upon themselves in 1920, con-
demning them to perpetual agonizing failure, when their then
owner, a theatrical producer named Harry Frazee, sold star
pitcher and slugger Babe Ruth—the Bambino—to the New York
Yankees. In 1946 the Red Sox, now a team of stars led by the
legendary Ted Williams, won their first American League
championship since 1918, but lost the World Series to the National League champion St. Louis Cardinals in the seventh and
deciding game under heartbreaking circumstances. Two years
later the Red Sox were tied for first place in the American
League at the end of the season, but lost in a one-game playoff
at their home Fenway Park. A year after that they entered
Yankee Stadium in New York needing to win only one of the last
two games of the season to become league champions, and lost
them both. All of this the young Bart Giamatti suffered through
at the end of seasons spent glued to the radio on summer
afternoons in South Hadley or at summer camp, following the
beloved Red Sox.

There were respects in which he stood apart from his peers.
He was intellectually inclined from the beginning, quick and
able in school, always a reader, often disappearing into his
personal domain—his room on the top floor in the Giamatti
house—to read in solitude. The Zane Grey novels were a favor-
ite, but he read anything he could lay his hands on. He possessed as a boy a verbal facility beyond that of others his age. As
a teenager he was an accomplished speaker and debater. He
won oratorical prizes at his high school. One Memorial Day he
was chosen from his Boy Scout troop to declaim the Gettys-
burg Address at the traditional annual ceremony on the town

common. At the boys camp in southern New Hampshire that
he attended for several summers, he edited and wrote for the
camp newspaper, the *Marienfeld Monitor,* exhibiting in his articles a breezy precocity unusual in a young teenager: at age
fourteen, for example, he advises his fellow campers that the
pitcher and catcher for Camp Marienfeld in an intercamp
baseball game were "through the fray the battery, the whole
battery, and nothing but the battery for our team." But despite
all these distinguishing talents, he was to his pals, even to his
siblings, an uncomplicated companion, just a normal kid like
the others.

His parents knew otherwise, for he was an unusually high-
strung child, with an active mind so bursting with nervous
energy that he sometimes had trouble sleeping. He was often
afflicted, until his mid-teens, with severe headaches requiring
special medication and periods of bed rest in a darkened room.
He was, his mother remembers, a very sensitive child, a worrier
even at a young age. His disposition, like his father's, was essentially sunny, but his sensitivity sometimes, as in later life,
manifested itself in a tendency to withdraw into himself and
internalize problems.

The Giamattis were a close family, largely without sibling
preferences or rivalries—"our parents let us be ourselves,"
Dino recalls. But Valentine Giamatti's relationship with and
influence on his elder son was particularly strong. Its intensity
can be partly accounted for by the natural affinity of a father
for his first son. They shared similarities in temperament: vol-
atile, verbal, warmly affectionate. These similarities deepened
as Bart Giamatti grew in appreciation of his Italian heritage.
Babbo became to his son Il Maestro—the Master. The Giamatti family spent two academic sabbatical years in Italy. After
the second, in 1954–55, Bart had achieved broad competence
in the Italian language, and when he entered Yale a year later,

after a preparatory year at Phillips Academy in Andover, Massachusetts, he began to apply this competence to studies that would lead him to an academic career in comparative literature with a strong Italian component. It would be too much to say that the career of the son mirrored that of his father. Renaissance English literature was the son's specialty; his father was principally a student and teacher of Dante. We have seen that Valentine Giamatti, free in a small women's college from the iron rule of "publish or perish," was not a productive scholar if measured by published output. His son was not yet thirty when his first important book was published, a study of the garden as a symbol in Western literature—dedicated to his mother and father. A second book—an introduction to Spenser's *Faerie Queene*—and various other writings followed before he left the life of scholarship for the presidency of Yale at the age of forty.

The father was never interested in academic administration. It can hardly be said that a man who progressed from modest immigrant circumstances to a distinguished academic career in a leading New England college lacked ambition—he certainly took advantage of every opportunity to improve himself. But he was comfortable in his good fortune; it was not his ambition to lead. His son, on the other hand, always had an agenda for leadership, in pursuit of which he was ambitious and competitive. Notwithstanding these important differences, the two had much to talk about intellectually, much to deepen the bonds between them. We sense how deep those bonds had become when we hear the son eulogizing the father after Valentine Giamatti's death in 1982:

> One of the last, and perhaps the most enduring, of the memories I have of my father is of him walking the beach in the full sun, a memory that is precise and clear and concrete and that is also a general figure for a life lived in every sense in the

open. . . . I shall always see him—in all the million ways we remember Babbo—as in the open, under an open sky; in the open sun which he loved as only one directly descended from the Etruscans by way of Naples can love the sun; with an open heart; and a mind always open—open to new people, new countries, new food, new languages, to new forms of human expression however they expressed themselves. . . . He was open above all to new ideas. He passionately believed in ideas and he spent his life thinking about how he could make ideas real, how he could connect the excitement in ideas he thought and felt to other people.

What a good life and what a good man. How that best of husbands and fathers and friends affirmed life for all of us and with all of us. How fortunate we all are to have walked the beach with him, at the full tide, in the sunshine he always made.

Andover

E ven before the Giamatti family sailed for Rome in the
fall of 1954 on sabbatical leave for the coming academic year, Bart's parents had concluded that South
Hadley High School had nothing further to give him educa-
tionally or socially, and that another school should be found for
his senior year in 1955–56. They chose Phillips Academy in
Andover, Massachusetts, the prestigious private school from
which Peggy's father, Bartlett Walton, had graduated. Application was made in early 1955, and on the basis of Bart's academic
record and favorable faculty assessments as a freshman and
sophomore at South Hadley High School and in his first se-
mester as a junior at the Overseas School of Rome, he was duly
admitted for the fall of that year.

Though Bart Giamatti had grown up next to the campus of
a small New England college, he must have been awed by what
he found at Andover. Around a central grass quadrangle inter-
sected by paved walks and bordered by Georgian brick administration and classroom buildings and dormitories was a vast
complex with every kind of facility for education, culture, and
sports. "Why not surround the boys with the very best in archi-

tecture and nature and the arts?" its principal designer had
asked. "Why not a bird sanctuary, a really fine library, a top-
notch art gallery, a good Colonial church with an organ? Why
not a few broad vistas, some lawns and terraces, even some
notable lectures and concerts—all the instruments of culture?"
It was all there and more. Bart had for the first time entered
an educational environment wholly conducive to the development of his intellectual promise.

Andover in the mid-1950s was still a school exclusively for
boys. The seven hundred or so students, almost all of them
boarders, lived in residential buildings, each presided over by a
faculty housemaster, and took their meals in a common dining
hall. Smoking was permitted in designated areas. Bart was
among the smokers: "We have given him permission to smoke
moderately," his father had reported in the parent memoran-
dum required by the school before matriculation. It was the
beginning of a destructive lifelong addiction to nicotine.

The adjustment to Andover was not always easy for a one-
year senior boarder who had previously lived at home, but
Bart's gregarious temperament and outgoing sense of humor
allowed him to adapt to his new environment with no apparent
difficulty. The hardest part of the adjustment was academic.
The prevalent standards at South Hadley High School and the
Overseas School of Rome, where Bart had made a very good
(though never brilliant) record, were not as rigorous as those at
Andover, an observation that was made repeatedly in the eval-
uations of his work by his teachers at the end of the fall term. It
is a credit to his perseverance and hard work that he made as
much progress as he did in overcoming these weaknesses.
When he graduated from Andover, he was (barely) in the top
quarter of his class. Continuing a pattern established in his
earlier high schools, he was best in English; his young English

teacher Ted Harrison thought him "the finest student I have ever taught." He was least successful in mathematics.

As at South Hadley, his extracurricular activities reflected his precocious verbal facility. He wrote for *The Phillipian*, the school newspaper. He joined Philo, the student debating society, in which he so distinguished himself as to be one of the six participants in the student prize debate and a member of the team that competed with other schools. *The Phillipian* praised his "peerless wit" as a debater. He was one of the winners in the student speaking competition and in the competition for original student essays.

All of these activities gave him prominence in the student body almost without precedent for a so-called PG—postgraduate student—the term applied to students attending Andover for a single year whether or not they were in fact postgraduates (most were, Giamatti was not). "Until Bart came along," a classmate has written, "non-jock [PGs] were invisible members of the senior class. His wit galvanized the student body." His visibility led to his election as a member of the Student Congress and as class secretary. He acquired a distinctive new nickname—Matts—that followed him with his Andover classmates long after graduation. But as the comment of his classmate suggests, he was specially recognized as an entertainer, the class wit. As a boy in South Hadley, Bart Giamatti the actor had entertained by impersonations. At Andover he invented for himself a new persona: the world-weary cynic. Here he is writing in *The Phillipian* on the return of students from the Christmas recess:

> As I sat in my acrid little room with my nose pressed against the cracked, dirty pane, I watched them return. Looking at the long files of returning boys, with their lean, debauched faces still sleepy with dissipation, I felt moved. . . .

Soon . . . the "Can You Top This" phase of the winter term
would begin. Orgies would be relived; boys would be men
again; New Years . . . Christmas . . . the first night home . . . all
this would be retold until the truth was out. Then the fun
would begin.

Or making a "report" as class secretary to an alumni luncheon:

I was impressed from the start with the courtesy angle of P.A.
life. An Andover man is courteous. So is a Boy Scout. So
what? Ah, but this is not the attitude. I was told an Andover
man is courteous and that courtesy is required of an Andover
man. I was obviously caught and so I too sunk, gleefully, into
the unfathomable pool of politeness.

The 1956 Andover year book includes a list of some fifty personal characteristics, each associated with a few seniors. It is
not surprising that the three characteristics ascribed to Giamatti are Original, Clown, and Cynical.

In reality this façade masked the genuine affection that
Giamatti had developed for Andover. "Andover was an extraordinary experience for me," he later said. "I met a whole new
range of people. I took superb courses. It was just the spirit of
the place I found so gripping and it meant an awful lot to me
later." We see the affection in the remarks Giamatti made at
the retirement dinner for his old English teacher Ted Harrison
in 1983, when Giamatti was president of Yale. The remarks
included a vignette from his student days, told with the generous humor of his mature style that contrasts vividly with the
mannered voice of the schoolboy. Harrison, a storied athlete at
Yale in his undergraduate days, was the Andover baseball
coach as well as an English teacher, and his second baseman in
Giamatti's year was a classmate named Tom Bagnoli. Giamatti
and Bagnoli were students in Harrison's 8:00 A.M. English
class, on this day busy with Wordsworth's "Intimations of Immortality." "Harrison had," Giamatti told the gathering,

a habit of throwing chalk, with either hand, from a sitting position, with superb control and without warning at students who were not working to a level he knew they could achieve. He never hit them with chalk, he only moved them back a little, the puffs of white dust from the explosion on the wall a reminder of the need to concentrate. They were brushback pitches designed, if you will, to encourage the batter to dig in. . . .

In the class, there was one Tom Bagnoli, . . . a fair second baseman. Good arm, fair moves, stylish without sweat. Now, Bagnoli—who was very bright—did not have a metabolism that was fully engaged at 8:00 A.M. Chalk was inefficacious with this scholar and at second base Bagnoli had seen more impressive missiles. And then one day, Harrison had had it. The gifted Bagnoli was not covering the bag and . . . the great Wordsworth, no swift baserunner but strong and purposeful, stole second on Bagnoli.

With a move whose speed and coherence I shall never forget, Harrison threw at Bagnoli—not chalk, not his glasses, not even the *Immortality Ode,* but the 11th Edition of Webster's Unabridged Dictionary . . . that sat by the teacher's right hand. . . . Some 30,000 words and plates, maps and indices, arced gracefully and accurately across the floor, the enormous book passing by those for whom it was not intended and finding, in the corner wedged in between the windows, the brave Bagnoli. . . . Bagnoli, now alert, caught the accumulated efforts of 700 years of English speaking people without great effort, only his face registering the shock of his teacher's and coach's skills.

Giamatti's affection for his old school manifested itself in many tangible ways. He remained as class secretary for an unusually long time, succeeding his own successor after a two-year interval and serving until the early 1970s. One of his last reports in that capacity reflected the fact that his Andover contemporaries were now thirtyish, with young families. "If you are around New Haven," he wrote as a rising Yale faculty member, in an appropriate variation on the class secretary's mandatory invitation to call when you're in town, "come by the Day Care Center and we will have juice."

For a period of three years in the 1970s Giamatti was an alumni trustee. And throughout his years at Yale, he took a deep interest in Andover graduates and did what he could to bring them to New Haven. Judith Sizer, Class of 1977, daughter of the then Headmaster Theodore Sizer, was one beneficiary of this interest. She has written that, undecided whether to attend Harvard or Yale, and encouraged by her parents to meet with Giamatti in New Haven, she was solemnly informed by him that she didn't want to go to Harvard, because "all there was in Cambridge were cheese shops. I really wanted . . . to go to Yale and . . . become an erudite professor of comparative literature like him. . . . How could I not go to Yale, after that?"

At the end of Giamatti's tenure as Yale's president, Andover reciprocated for all his services to the school by presenting to him its annual award for distinguished contribution to public service.

Yale

There was never any question that Bart Giamatti and his family intended for him to go to Yale, his father's school, after his year at Andover. His scholastic record at Andover, together with faculty recommendations emphasizing his capacity for leadership and intellectual promise, insured that he would be admitted. The Yale he entered as a freshman in the fall of 1956 looked far different from the college his father had entered a generation earlier. During the 1930s ten new residential colleges had been completed, those in the center of the campus built in a heavy granite neo-Gothic style that complemented the imposing Harkness Tower and the Sterling Memorial Library, also Gothic, to give the college a predominant new architectural unity.

Yale was, on the surface at least, in other respects serenely traditional. The disruptions and overcrowding of the war years were now in the distant past, and the college was much as it had been in Valentine Giamatti's day. More than half of the students still came from private schools, most of them in the Northeast. The observation of the dean of Yale College, William C. DeVane, in his 1948 report to the president of the university was still valid: "The activities of our students—athletic, social, managerial, commercial—are so attractive that they all but overwhelm the intellectual aspects of a college education." Dean DeVane had gone on to express the hope that this would change:

> What I want for Yale College is an intellectual eminence as great as her athletic or her social or her eminence in activities of all sorts. . . . I would have Yale turn out more leaders of the intellectual life of our country. For the man of action we unquestionably provide a superb training—none better. For the man of intellectual achievement I am afraid that we are surpassed by Harvard, Columbia and Chicago.

It was 1962 before this sentiment found a decisive echo, in the Report of the President's Committee on the Freshman Year, chaired by Professor Leonard W. Doob:

> We must view the whole educational process as a more mature and serious undertaking not only for those students who will join the learned professions, but also for those who will enter business, industry or government. . . . It is incumbent upon Yale and similar institutions consciously to increase the number of learned men in our society. . . . Candidates whose records show exceptionally high promise of continuing intellectual achievement should be sought out and admitted without regard for any other criteria save those indicative of emotional maturity and good character.

Three more years passed before this goal began to be achieved, in the first of the three revolutions at Yale in the 1960s: a change in admissions policy under President Kingman Brewster's new dean of admissions, R. Inslee Clark, Jr., that emphasized intellectual achievement and promise over social background. The result, unpopular with many alumni, was that the percentage of the freshman class coming from public high schools rose from 44 percent in 1960 to 58 percent a decade later, and the representation of sons of Yale graduates over the same period dropped from 24 percent to 12 percent. Brewster was quoted as saying, "I do not intend to preside over a finishing school on Long Island Sound." The injured feelings of disappointed alumni were not soothed.

Signs of the second of the revolutions at Yale in the 1960s— the rise of student protests associated with the civil rights movement and opposition to the war in Vietnam, accompanied by the emergence of a counterculture of disaffected youth— were scarcely in evidence in the mid-1950s. The students of that time were part of the so-called silent generation, pervaded, it was said, by apathy. Looking back from the vantage point of the 1970s, Giamatti himself thought he detected, instead of apathy, an "intense skepticism," prefiguring a later rebellious student generation, when "the fifties' desire for something more coherent and purposeful would [become] the sixties' battle cry of Illegal, Immoral, Unjust." But it is hard to avoid the conclusion that this is the wisdom of hindsight.

The Doob report also asserted that "Yale has a national duty, as well as a duty to itself, to provide the rigorous training for women that we provide for men." To this end it contained what it called a "long-range recommendation" that women should be admitted to Yale as undergraduates, but it acknowledged that this was a possibility "requiring further study and lying beyond the realm of present practicality." This recommendation was finally implemented in 1969, in the last of the revolutions at Yale in the 1960s, when the first undergraduate class including women entered the college.

Giamatti lived during his freshman year on the Old Campus in Vanderbilt Hall with three roommates from his Andover class, Tom Crosby, Moose McKamy, and Haj Ross. It was an uneventful year at Yale. Adlai Stevenson, now forgotten but then the darling of academia, visited the campus in the fall during the presidential campaign that was to end in his second defeat by Dwight Eisenhower. Billy Graham came in the spring. The Suez Crisis and the Soviet suppression of the Hungarian revolution dominated the news from abroad, but they were far away. Perhaps the greatest excitement at Yale during the 1956–57 academic year was provided by the varsity football team, which had its most successful season since the war, beating Princeton 42-20 and Harvard 44-14. Giamatti took a standard curriculum, with the success that started him on the way to graduation three years later magna cum laude. As at Andover, his wit made him visible. He was elected a member of the Freshman Prom Committee and the Undergraduate Affairs Committee.

After the freshman year, Yale undergraduates move into one of the residential colleges. Giamatti's was Saybrook, located in the heart of the campus on Elm Street. There he lived for his last three college years. In the late 1950s, Yale students led quiet lives, though at the time they would surely not have acknowledged it. Guest celebrities came and went, many of them invited by a new organization called Challenge, which urged the Yale community to "confront with realistic concern and responsible action the crucial issues of today's world" and became the focal point of debate about current events and the threat of the nuclear bomb. With the advent of Challenge, the student historian of the Class of 1960 wrote, "we were no longer free to vegetate. Our cherished inalienable right to apathy, to indifference, to non-think, was challenged." But the quiet prevailed nonetheless. Classes, exams, and weekend parties also came and went.

In his junior year, Giamatti chose to major in English, and his academic success continued. But success, which he coveted, did not always come easily or without emotional cost. Alvin Kernan, in his memoir of life in the academy, *In Plato's*

Cave, offers a vignette revealing that under the jaunty insouciance Giamatti customarily showed to the outside world was a strong and quite serious need for approval:

> Bart was a student in the Yale honors program when I was a young teacher. I thought his first paper overwritten, illogical, and generally pompous, and said so. I concluded my lengthy remarks on the paper with the advice: "You must learn to write more simply and directly if you wish to achieve success in any field." Bart was a very cool fellow, popular, exchanging easy jokes with anyone and everyone—"Hey, paisano!"—but within minutes after I had put the paper outside my door he was pounding on it, crushed and angry.

The single dramatic exception to the serenity of life at Yale during Giamatti's undergraduate years, significant for what it tells us about town-gown relations in the New Haven of that era, was a pair of episodes in March 1959 that came to be called the snowball riots. Several inches of snow in the middle of the month occasioned the first episode, a campuswide snowball fight late on a Thursday evening planned by students. The disturbance spilled over into the New Haven streets, requiring the intervention of the city police, some of whom used excessive force. Unfortunately, the annual St. Patrick's Day parade was scheduled for the following Saturday, and many students were still angry at what they perceived as mistreatment by the police. As the parade, including, Kernan recalls, "the drum and bugle corps of many Catholic schools and brigades of Irish lassies with bare white legs and short green skirts twirling their batons," proceeded up Elm Street past the Yale campus, escorted by policemen on foot and on motorcycles, snowballs were thrown and verbal insults were exchanged. Violence again broke out, made worse by resentment at the interruption by Yale students of an occasion for the expression of civic pride, national and religious. It was a reprise of a similar episode only seven years earlier. Both were still fresh memories two decades later when Giamatti, as president of Yale, the son of a second generation Italian immigrant born and raised in New Haven, was making it a priority of his administration to improve relations with the community.

Perhaps Giamatti's closest friend at Yale was Dan Catlin, who lived across Elm Street in Trumbull College. It had not taken young Bart Giamatti long to discover that he was welcome in the Italian neighborhoods of New Haven that had known his father. Catlin became a beneficiary of this discovery. Wanting perhaps to expose his friend, born to privilege and raised in Manhattan, to a wider world, Giamatti took Catlin along on his frequent visits to the Wooster Street section of the city, now gentrified and fully accessible to Yale students, but then an unwelcoming place for most Yale students.

Catlin particularly admired Giamatti's strong independent streak. He went his own way and developed friends across a broad spectrum of campus constituencies far beyond his Andover classmates—athletes, theater people, serious students. When the time came in sophomore year to join a fraternity, he chose Delta Kappa Epsilon, the haven for jocks, over the more traditional prep school fraternities, like the Fence Club and Zeta Psi. Unlike most of his classmates, who reacted passively to what they were asked to study, Giamatti had strong opinions about the contents of his courses. Catlin remembers the literature class taught by Yale professor Charles Feidelson, for example, when he developed and expressed vigorously a strong dislike for Thomas Mann's novel *The Magic Mountain*.

Giamatti was active in a raft of organizations. In his senior year he was chairman of the Yale Charities Drive, revealing again the ambition for visibility that had placed him as a freshman on the Undergraduate Affairs Committee. He was active in the Yale Dramat, with, as we shall see, profound consequences for his later life. He was a member of the Pundits, ten undergraduates supposed to be Yale's greatest wits, who met regularly for lunch and sparkling conversation. He was elected to the Elizabethan Club, that singular Yale institution possessed of a tidy white house on College Street that holds a priceless collection of rare books, including a Shakespeare First Folio and several quartos, where tea and sandwiches are served to student and faculty members on weekday afternoons in a setting conducive to serious conversation. He was one of fifteen members of the prestigious Aurelian Honor Society in his senior year.

In the spring of his junior year, Giamatti, together with fourteen other members of the Class of 1960, accepted an invitation to join Scroll and Key, one of the oldest of Yale's senior societies. Scroll and Key was formed in 1842, at a time that has been called "the flowering of New England," before the horrors of the Civil War and the aggressive competitive environment of the Gilded Age that followed it. It was the heyday of Ralph Waldo Emerson, the apostle of the nobility of the individual will, who preached that "Truth, and goodness, and beauty, are but different faces of the same All," and that men could seek them "without effeminacy." These ideals were to be pursued in the new society through ritual and a program of literary exercises in the privacy of a fellowship kept apart from the outside world.

Giamatti's group possessed the diversity that enriches the experience in Scroll and Key. Of the fifteen, five were captains of a varsity sport in their senior year (baseball, crew, tennis, wrestling, football); six earned academic distinction of some sort. Catlin was among them. Each was assigned a traditional identity; Giamatti, as might have been expected, was one of the two funny men. Meetings were held weekly in the society's hall on College Street, with a dinner followed by the program. By

Giamatti's time the rituals, modified and enhanced from their beginnings, had been long settled: songs and a certain pattern of informal foolery. The original literary exercises, which for a time had centered on the plays of Shakespeare, had assumed a more broadly intellectual form. In this environment of mixed conviviality and seriousness, the element of fellowship that has characterized the society from its earliest days continued.

His time in Scroll and Key was for Giamatti, as it is for most members, a high point of his undergraduate years. Long afterward, he recalled it as an experience in "self-education, where an individual learns about how an individual lives in a group, and how a group lives with ideals conveyed by an institution, . . . and out of that study, [learns] lessons of respect for, service to, and affection with, others." Giamatti remained an active participant in the affairs of Scroll and Key during all his years at Yale and thereafter. A defining characteristic of the society throughout its long life has been its financial support of Yale at many times and in many ways. On more than one occasion, instances of that support have occurred in recognition of milestones in Giamatti's own career.

Giamatti's Yale class graduated in June 1960. He delivered the class oration. It betrays some of the pomposity that Professor Kernan had criticized, without the light touch that mixes with high seriousness in Giamatti's speeches as an adult. But he says some interesting things that suggest later preoccupations. The apathy that afflicts his generation is, he says, not a disease but a symptom; the disease is the lack of a unifying body of belief. Some people compensate for this void by what Giamatti calls "the Busy reaction," which he says is no less dangerous to the individual than passivity. The Busy reaction is "to be always involved with involvement, to be terribly—finally, irrevocably—committed to commitment." He urges looking to the past, "not with an eye to returning to . . . some lost Eden, but with an eye to re-evaluating yesterday so that we will be able to fashion a creed, a myth, for uncertain tomorrows." Giamatti was never a man for causes—of the Left or of the Right. Even as an undergraduate, he sensed that the lessons of the past are more valuable than the preoccupations of the present.

We have seen that one of Giamatti's undergraduate activities was the Yale Dramat. In his junior year he played a minor role in a production in which the leading lady was Toni Smith, a pretty blonde aspiring actress studying in the Yale Drama School. A romance blossomed, followed by a courtship privately conducted—no one could remember any double dates—and by Giamatti's senior year the two were engaged. Catlin says that as a senior Giamatti's major goal was to finish college so he could marry Toni Smith. He did so a week after graduation in her hometown of Plainfield, New Jersey. Catlin, who was an usher, remembers that it was a simple affair, "not a blow-out event; . . . it just happened and life went on."

In his class yearbook, Giamatti had written that after college he planned to pursue "graduate work in comparative literature, possibly at Harvard." He was, in fact, not admitted there, a rebuff he never spoke about and never forgot. He was accepted at Yale, however, so the couple returned to New Haven and settled into an apartment in nearby Branford. He entered graduate school in the fall of 1960, and by the spring of 1964 he had completed his course work and his doctoral dissertation on the garden as a symbol in Renaissance literature, later published in reworked form as his first book, *The Earthly Paradise and the Renaissance Epic*. By this time the Giamattis had two children, a son Marcus born in October 1961 and a daughter Elena born in March 1964. There was no teaching job available at the time at Yale, but one was offered at Princeton, so in the fall of 1964 Giamatti and his family left New Haven to take up his first academic post there.

Princeton

The Giamatti family moved into an apartment in a housing complex for young faculty overlooking Lake Carnegie on the Princeton campus, and Bart took up his teaching duties. He taught the beginning course in Italian and served as the leader (preceptors they are called at Princeton) of one of the small discussion groups in the large introductory course for freshmen on European literature. He was an instant success. In an evaluation prepared near the end of the first term, the chairman of the Department of Romance Languages and Literature, Edward Sullivan, reported to the dean of the faculty that Giamatti was a "first-rate Instructor in Italian," an "excellent preceptor . . . highly regarded by . . . the head of the course," and overall "a first-rate teacher, warm, dedicated, and stimulating." "A very promising young man," the report concluded, "well grounded in his subject, alert and vigorous, he is at the beginning of what will surely be a very fine career." Giamatti had been hired as an instructor on a three-year appointment. The evaluation was accompanied by a recommendation that he be promoted to the rank of assistant professor in the coming academic year. The recommendation was favorably acted upon.

Meanwhile, Giamatti and his family settled into Princeton life. The fall was clouded by the near-fatal illness with meningitis of their three-year-old son Marcus. The boy received adequate care in the local hospital and made a full recovery, but Giamatti was uneasy about the absence of a sophisticated teaching hospital of the kind that would have come with a first-class medical school. He already thought of himself as in "exile" from his true home at Yale, and the experience with Marcus intensified that feeling. As would always be the case, the Giamatti family did not entertain or socialize. But the gregarious Bart made many friends, chief among them his colleague Robert Hollander, a budding Dante specialist five years Giamatti's senior, at the beginning of a long career at Princeton that would establish him as one of America's leading *dantisti*. The two men became inseparable, lunching together two or three times a week to discuss and argue about the fine points of *The Divine Comedy*. In his second academic year at Princeton, Giamatti added to his teaching duties the role of preceptor and guest lecturer in a course given by Hollander on Dante, Cervantes, and Goethe.

But Giamatti remained unhappy at Princeton. He told friends that his eight years in New Haven had made him "a flea on the belly of Mother Yale," and he wanted to go back. Maynard Mack, then chairman of the Yale English department, had sounded him out in his first year at Princeton about returning to Yale, but Giamatti, newly promoted to assistant professor, thought it would be unseemly to leave so soon and under those circumstances. But when Mack called again on a fall Friday in 1965 with the offer of an assistant professorship commencing in the 1966–67 academic year, Giamatti decided that the time had come. Mack knew that Princeton would fight back, and he told Giamatti he wanted an answer by the following Monday. Over the weekend Chairman Sullivan moved heaven and earth to produce a proposal that Hollander says was the best deal ever offered to an assistant professor, accompanied by a personal interview with the president of the university: immediate promotion to associate professor with tenure, and the promise of a full professorship after the briefest interval that academic decencies would permit. But Giamatti had made up his mind, and the chairman was obliged to write the president that "in spite of all our efforts Bart Giamatti has decided to accept the post of Assistant Professor at Yale. He was pleased to have had a chance to talk with you, but it was clear practically from the beginning that nothing could keep him here at this time."

The chairman concluded with the thought that "we may well be making efforts in a few years to bring him back here," and in 1974 Princeton tried, offering Giamatti, by this time a full professor of English and comparative literature at Yale, the post of chairman of its Humanities Center. He treated the offer with respect, spending time in Princeton to learn about it, perhaps as a courtesy to Hollander and to his old Yale teacher and faculty colleague Alvin Kernan, then at Princeton as dean of its graduate school, who had made the offer. But he never seriously considered it. He had left Princeton for good in 1966, returning only in 1978 to accept the honorary degree that Princeton customarily confers on presidents of Yale. "Although he taught here only briefly," the citation concluded, "Princeton can now claim a new alumnus who brings abundant capacities of mind and spirit to the leadership of higher education."

His last night in Princeton, Giamatti had dinner with Bob Hollander. It was a bittersweet occasion. "It'll never be the same, Bart," said Hollander as they walked out to Giamatti's car at the end of the evening. "Aw, c'mon, Hollander," Giamatti replied, "we'll always be friends." But Hollander was right; it would—could—never be the same. And there were tears in his eyes as he turned back to his house.

Yale:
Scholar and Teacher

Yale in the 1960s and 1970s

So in the fall of 1966 Giamatti and his family were back in New Haven, settled into a modest house in the Westville section of the city near the Yale Bowl. As Maynard Mack later boasted, Yale had been "able to disengage him from the lotus-eating life of Princeton and bring him home to the rocky Ithaca that Yale has always been, where only snow foxes and mountain goats survive."

The Yale to which Giamatti returned was different from the Yale he had left two years earlier; it was already moving in the direction of the emotional and disorderly environment that would become known as "the sixties." Two episodes that had occurred in Giamatti's absence signaled this movement. The first illustrated the central place that opposition to the war in Vietnam would occupy in the new environment. In December 1965 a young assistant professor of history named Staughton Lynd accompanied the American Communist historian Herbert Aptheker and the California-based political activist Tom Hayden on what they called a "fact-finding mission" to Hanoi, the capital of North Vietnam. While he was there, Lynd stated publicly his belief that the Johnson administration had lied to the American people and that U.S. policy in Vietnam was "immoral, illegal, and antidemocratic." Upon his return to Yale, Lynd gave an account of his trip to a capacity audience of three thousand in the university's largest auditorium, at the end of which he received a standing ovation.

Lynd's trip tested to the limit the position of Yale's president, Kingman Brewster, asserted only the month before in a speech to the Yale Club of Southern California, "that as long as I am convinced that a man is conscientious, as long as I am convinced that he is not in default with respect to his teaching and scholarly obligations for which he is employed, then the long-run interests of this university . . . make it unthinkable that we should penalize a faculty member for his political position." Consistent with this policy Lynd was not penalized by Yale. Brewster's public comment on the incident was limited to criticism of Lynd's having given aid and comfort to a government engaged in hostilities with American forces by disparaging his country's leadership and policies while in Hanoi.

The other episode that marked the changing environment at Yale, which also occurred in 1965, involved not the war in Vietnam but a question of faculty promotion. In March of that year it was announced that Richard J. Bernstein, an associate professor in the philosophy department, serving on term without tenure, would not be awarded tenure and would be leaving Yale. Bernstein was an immensely popular teacher, and his failure to achieve tenure illustrated dramatically the tension in a research university between the dual tenure criteria of strong teaching and first-rate technical scholarship. A student protest meeting was soon organized, followed by a round-the-clock picketing vigil outside the Woodbridge Hall offices of President Brewster, lasting more than seventy-two consecutive hours. Brewster took the unusual step of inquiring into the basis for the decision by the relevant appointments committee.

The inquiry brought to light the previously undisclosed fact that the recommendation for tenure by Bernstein's own department had been qualified, and it was soon withdrawn, thereby effectively putting an end to the matter. Brewster initiated a faculty review of tenure criteria, during which students were invited to make their views known, and the episode was over. But Yale had seen a dramatic instance of growing consciousness by students of their own interests and the power of organized dissent. This power was to be exercised with increasing frequency and intensity in the years ahead.

Protests remained peaceful at Yale until 1969. When a silent "vigil" for peace in Vietnam was planned to coincide with a visit to the campus in the fall of 1967 by Lady Bird Johnson, the president's wife, to speak on "The Beautification of America," organizers insisted that the protest be orderly and that "every courtesy" be shown the first lady. An antiwar march of five thousand protestors through downtown New Haven the following year led by Yale chaplain William Sloane Coffin, Jr., and the playwright Arthur Miller went off without incident; the organizers praised the police for their cooperation in keeping the demonstration peaceful. But by the spring of 1969 things were turning ugly.

The change in tone coincided with a new activism by the Yale chapter of Students for a Democratic Society (SDS), formed in 1967 but quiet until encouraged by SDS uprisings on other Ivy League campuses. The first of these occurred in the spring of 1968 at Columbia, where SDS protests against the university's plan, opposed by black groups, to build a gymnasium in Harlem led to occupation by students of several university buildings and an ensuing police "bust" that radicalized the campus. This incident was followed by a reenactment of the Columbia scenario at Harvard a year later, in early April 1969, when the occupation by students of an administration building in protest of the ROTC program on campus, again instigated by SDS, followed by forcible action to clear it by local police (not a Harvard man among them), led to a student and faculty strike that paralyzed the university.

Less than two weeks later SDS at Yale, under pressure as a result of what had happened at Harvard, acted. Earlier in the year the faculty had reviewed the status of the ROTC and had voted to discontinue academic credit for its courses. But a contingent of students, led by SDS, insisted that Yale had not gone far enough. A mass meeting of students was called, at which it was voted to "request" that the ROTC be denied access to all university property. The Brewster administration reacted calmly, calling meetings of students and faculty as the beginning of a process that ultimately led to a further modification of Yale's relationship with the ROTC. SDS was not successful in creating an environment of violent confrontation, and the issue subsided.

But the prospect of further student unrest remained, and Brewster, responding to an overwhelming faculty sentiment that physical coercion had no place on the Yale campus, announced a policy to deal with it: outside authorities would be called in to quell a student disruption only as a last resort, after the exhaustion of a process that moved from an offer of consultation, to a warning of suspension, to suspension itself, to enforcement by the campus police, and, finally, to legal action. The policy was put to the test the following month, when SDS organized an invasion of the Yale treasurer's office to protest anew the ROTC program. In accordance with the Brewster scenario, the students were offered a meeting with administration officials and, when that was refused, they were told they would be suspended if they did not leave by a specified time. They left peaceably.

By the fall of 1969 Yale was congratulating itself that it did not "blow" in the face of SDS provocation. But the smugness was premature. In November of that year Colia Williams, a black waitress working for a thirty-day trial period in one of the college dining halls, was discharged following an incident involving alleged insubordination. A large group of students occupied the university's personnel offices in Wright Hall and refused to leave until Williams was reinstated. This time they did not respond to a threat of suspension, and forty-seven of them were suspended forthwith, the term and conditions of their suspension to be determined by the executive committee of Yale College, which at that time included student representatives. The committee took the matter under advisement, and, while requiring formal withdrawal of the students as a matter of record, "in view of the fact that the events in Wright Hall constituted an unprecedented situation at Yale" recommended immediate reinstatement, subject to probation for the rest of the academic year. The recommendation, which carried with it a warning that any future incident would result in permanent suspension, was considered at a meeting of the full faculty. A motion to reject it put forward by members who thought it too lenient was decisively defeated, and the committee's recommendation was accepted. If SDS was looking for a stark confrontation with the university over the issue of "amnesty" for offenders, always a sympathetic one among students, Brewster's Yale did not give it to them.

The turmoil of the sixties at Yale culminated in the events of the first weekend of May 1970—the so-called May Day crisis. Like the Wright Hall episode, the issue was civil rights rather than the war, though many antiwar activists participated and the situation was certainly worsened by President Nixon's announcement the last week in April of increased military aid for an invasion of Cambodia. But the confrontation on May Day was not over something as uncomplicated as the rights of a fired black waitress in a university dining hall. It was about the civil rights movement in its most dramatic form: the threat of violence in the name of Black Power.

In the late summer of 1969, Bobby Seale, national chairman of the Black Panther Party, was arrested with several others and charged with having ordered the killing in New Haven the previous spring of Alex Rackley, a party member suspected by other members of being a police informant. As the date for Seale's trial approached in the spring of 1970, representatives of the Black Panthers and other radicals appeared in New Haven to organize support for freeing Seale, efforts that found a defining moment in a mass rally at Yale's Ingalls Rink, at which a Panther leader explicitly called for violence against law enforcement officials ("pigs") and Yale pacifists who supported them. The tension was broken by a bizarre incident, the sudden appearance on stage of an apparently confused young man in a white shirt, who had been roughed up by Panther bodyguards. He took the microphone and stood silent for several minutes, occasionally mumbling incoherently, before being led away by a faculty member. The meeting, de-energized, broke up without incident, and students returned to their colleges, most of which voted to strike in support of Seale.

At a meeting the following day, the faculty and administration in effect accepted the strike, voting to "modify" normal academic activities, including the expectation that instructors would meet their classes. It was at this meeting that President Brewster made the statement many alumni and others remember as the keynote of May Day. Brewster had insisted from the start of the crisis that Yale should remain neutral on the issue of Seale's guilt or innocence, should do what it could to insure a fair trial for Seale and his codefendants, and should try to prevent violence. He did not retreat from these principles, but he went on to say, "I am appalled and ashamed that things should have come to such a pass that I am skeptical of the ability of black revolutionaries to achieve a fair trial anywhere in the United States." This statement cost Brewster support among conservative alumni that left him seriously weakened when Yale faced a financial crisis later in the 1970s.

After this, May Day itself was something of an anticlimax. The Brewster administration wisely chose to treat visitors to New Haven in support of the rally organized by the Panther Defense Fund Committee as guests rather than invaders. Food, lodging, and meeting facilities were offered, and access to the campus was permitted. The Yale community, long loyal to Brewster for his outspoken opposition to the war in Vietnam and support for the rights of blacks, rallied behind him. Even the Black Panthers became advocates for nonviolence, and the events of the weekend passed without serious incident. On Sunday afternoon Brewster was able to express his "admiration and gratitude" to everyone concerned with keeping the peace. "We licked them with love," said Chaplain Coffin. New Haven remained peaceful throughout Seale's trial, which ended more than a year later when all charges against him were dropped after a jury could not reach a verdict.

May Day brought together at Yale the twin causes of civil rights, in the particularly dangerous form of the Black Panthers, and of withdrawal from Vietnam, in the form of many veteran activists. But a third major impulse of the day was also present, the "youth movement" or "counterculture," represented by two of its leading apostles, Abbie Hoffman and Jerry Rubin, preaching the incongruent goals of revolution and "dropping out." Here is Hoffman speaking at Yale during the days leading up to May Day:

Work—W-O-R-K—is a dirty four-letter word. . . . We need a society in which work and play are not separate. We gotta destroy the Protestant Ethic as well as capitalism, racism, imperialism—that's gotta go too. We want a society in which dancin' in the streets isn't separate from cuttin' sugar cane—
. . . We have picked the Yale lock.

All of this turmoil washed around the young Giamatti as it did around all of Yale. What did he think of it? He has been portrayed by some as a hawk on Vietnam and—even worse—a conservative Republican. There is little evidence for either portrayal. "I am an independent voter and always have been," he told an interviewer after his election as Yale's president. "I don't know whether I have ever voted a straight ticket. . . . What looks pretty conservative in an academic community like Yale does not necessarily look very conservative somewhere else."

But whatever his politics, Giamatti was appalled at the confrontations, full of shouted slogans and the threat of violence, by which political opinions were being expressed. The ideal university, which he described in a memorable series of speeches to students during his presidency of Yale, must be a "free and ordered space"; those who would coerce others, on the Left or on the Right, are "terrorists of the mind." There is no freedom without order: "A civilized order is the precondition of freedom, and freedom . . . the goal of responsible order." As for Giamatti's view of the youth movement, we may infer his disapproval from his description of it years later:

This was not so much a "movement" as a state of mind, a state of mind embodied in a certain kind of music, hair and dress. Beads, bells, country-style dress, single names, "grass"—a whole world of pastoral assumptions and accoutrements accompanied this impulse, including a kind of humorless ag-

gressive innocence, an absolutist social morality, and an un-
shakable conviction that authenticity resided in a seeming
lack of artifice.

Yet for all his disdain—contempt would hardly be too strong
a word—for the values of the sixties, Giamatti looked upon the
students who embraced them as individual works in progress
entitled to every benefit of the doubt, as victims rather than
offenders. He must have disapproved strongly of the conduct of
the SDS students who occupied Wright Hall in 1969 in support
of a black waitress, but when the motion came at a faculty
meeting to reject the recommendation of the executive committee for leniency, he voted against it and in favor of accepting
the recommendation. In perhaps his angriest writing about the
sixties, an attack on the so-called Free Speech Movement,
"where we first began to hear language mediated through the
bullhorn into the formulaic chant of a crowd," and its disastrous effect on the linguistic skills of a generation, he says of the
students who were its victims that they were "lied to."

It has been the custom at Scroll and Key for each class to
have its photograph taken as a group, traditionally in dark suits
and a solemn pose. This custom was caricatured by the groups
of the sixties. Giamatti's sense of where the blame lay for what
he believed to be their misplaced values is apparent from his
description of the picture of the Class of 1971. In it, he writes,

> the role playing in which college students have been encour-
> aged to engage—playing the parts of Wholly Idealistic Young
> and Moral Guardians, roles thrust on them by elders who
> knew better, or should have—has now taken over. . . . Here
> each man has literally struck a pose, taken a role, "done his
> own thing," and the overall impression, because of the dif-
> ferent styles of dress and the different postures, is of disparate
> individuals, . . . with as many avoiding the camera's gaze as

meeting it, the hilarity forced, the poses not quite taking, the whole not really cohering at all. It is the saddest picture, at least to this viewer, on the wall.

The same attitude of resigned sadness over a misled student generation emerges clearly from a vignette provided by Alan Bernheimer, a graduate of Yale College in the Class of 1970. Giamatti had been the instructor in his freshman English course. Like so many of Giamatti's students, Bernheimer has rich praise for him as a teacher ("I don't recall being as challenged in any of my subsequent literature courses"), but it is his brief contact with Giamatti later in his college career that is relevant here:

> I didn't have much formal contact with Mr. Giamatti after my freshman year, but do recall a cameo a few years later as I was walking through the Saybrook common room, most likely in purple bell-bottoms and possibly flowered shirt, and he looked up in his academic tweeds, pipe in hand, and shook his head ruefully, smiling, "Ah, Bernheimer."

It must have been a cigarette rather than a pipe, but the tone of forgiving tolerance is unmistakable.

The May Day weekend was effectively the end of the sixties at Yale. The war in Vietnam dragged on until 1973, and there were occasional protest rallies, all peaceful. But the energy was gone, dissipated in part, certainly, by the winding down of the draft beginning at the end of 1969. New issues were coming to the fore that were to dominate the rest of the century. Affirmative action was one, affecting both faculty and students, accompanied by the founding of an Afro-American Studies program. Political correctness was another, though as yet only vaguely discernible: it was still possible in 1974 for a campus group to sponsor a debate including William Shockley, the

Stanford physics professor who was a proponent of a theory of black genetic inferiority, and for the university to discipline students who disrupted it during the turbulence that it created. The report of a committee appointed by President Brewster to develop a policy on freedom of expression at Yale asserted, with only limited dissent, that the university's primary function of disseminating knowledge requires the free interchange of ideas, and without sacrificing this function "it cannot make its primary and dominant value the fostering of friendship, solidarity, harmony, civility or mutual respect."

Militant feminism was still in the future, but the place of women at Yale was a matter of intense debate and concern in the early 1970s. An important goal of coeducation, as recommended in the Doob report, was that women should not be admitted "on a token basis," but only five hundred women were in the first coeducational class in 1969, representing slightly more than 10 percent of the total enrollment in Yale College. It was 1972 before the university committed itself to a program that had as its goal the creation of a 60-40 ratio of men to women, and almost the end of the decade before that ratio was achieved. Today men and women are represented about equally in Yale College.

Evidence of the change of priorities at Yale in the 1970s was the scant attention paid to the resignation in early 1975 of the controversial university chaplain, William Sloane Coffin, Jr., after seventeen years. Coffin had first gained prominence as a civil rights activist in the South. But it was his radical opposition to the war in Vietnam that galvanized Yale students and faculty in the late 1960s. Coffin led marches. He preached resistance to the draft. He was indicted on charges of conspiring to aid draft resisters, and convicted by a Boston jury before being freed on appeal. He was a hero of the activists of the sixties. And now he was leaving quietly because he thought nothing very creative was going on at Yale. He was bored. "The wings of my spirit," he said, "need to be exercised."

Constantly present at Yale in the 1970s were two intractable issues that poisoned the atmosphere: labor unrest and a financial crisis. The custodial and maintenance workers struck for higher wages and better working conditions in 1971 for fifty days and again in 1974 and 1977 for even longer periods, seriously disrupting campus life, especially for students. The financial crisis, which dominated Giamatti's presidency and is therefore properly the subject for detailed consideration in a later chapter, affected primarily the faculty. Commencing in 1972 budget cuts totaling 20 percent were imposed over a three-year period. "In New Haven, in the faculty, in the early to middle seventies," Giamatti has written, "it seemed as if it were raining every day."

It was the faculty, too, that was most affected by a new revolution of the seventies, generically called postmodernism, an intellectual sequel to the social revolution of the sixties that questioned traditional orthodoxies in all phases of the arts. In literature this movement took the form of a radical philosophy known as deconstruction, which holds that a "play" of linguistic "signs" in a text operates to obliterate the distinction between what has been thought "marginal" and a stabilizing "center," upon which traditional textual interpretation depends. What is the center, the deconstructionist asks, if the marginal can become central? Thus the identifying rubric of the deconstruction movement: all interpretation is misinterpretation.

Giamatti, the scholar and teacher of the Renaissance, where mutability is a recurrent theme, was certainly aware of the instability of language, of words as a means of illusion and deceit. We will see it particularly in his writings on Edmund Spenser, who memorably created in *The Faerie Queene* a goddess named Mutability, and gave her dominion over all earthly things. *A Play of Double Senses* is the title of Giamatti's principal study of Spenser. But no postmodernist, he was certainly unsympathetic to the deconstructionists, who, he said dismissively, had "made a little machine, an endlessly wearing blender," to prove that language is inherently deceptive. For Giamatti, to deny language, for all its capacity to deceive, was to deny history. "Without a respect for its awesome power," he wrote in 1976, "we can never find out who we are, and thus never leave the child's garden of feeling and enter the city—that is, become citizens."

In these confusions of the 1960s and 1970s the Giamatti family continued to live in New Haven while Giamatti pursued his career as a scholar and teacher. There was now a third child, Paul, born in 1967. Toni Giamatti had begun a career as a teacher of English at Hopkins Grammar Day Prospect Hill School in New Haven, attended by the Giamatti children and the children of many other Yale academics. Giamatti himself now sported a moustache and a goatee, a combination often seen in portraits of Renaissance princes—a new identifying persona.

Academic advancement came regularly. He was promoted to the rank of associate professor in 1968 and made a full professor two years later. He became the Frederick Clifford Ford Professor of English and Comparative Literature in 1976. When, the following year, Yale established the John Hay Whitney Professorship in the Humanities, with an endowment based upon an initial gift of $100,000 by Scroll and Key in honor of its old member, the distinguished Yale benefactor, Giamatti became its first holder.

In the 1970s Giamatti undertook a series of administrative assignments. The first of these was the position of master of Ezra Stiles College, beginning in 1970. The family rented the house in Westville and moved into the master's lodgings. Giamatti threw himself into his duties and was by all accounts a successful master, but he resigned the post after two years, restive in a position that inevitably meant a loss of privacy and a dilution of scholarly activity. He and his wife were also concerned that a large house full of spirited undergraduates was not a suitable environment for young children. It was not the last time the ambitious Giamatti took on a major assignment without accurately gauging his suitability for it and the personal cost.

It was during his mastership that the episode occurred which has given rise to an anecdote that is a staple of the Giamatti canon. As it is told by his great friend Donald Kagan:

> In the course of the question and answer period [during a Parents Weekend], a woman got up and said, "I've just been to see my son's room and it's a mess and his roommates' rooms are a mess; the entryways are all terribly messy. Can you explain that to me?" Bart adopted the tone he sometimes did in public—an 18th-century Samuel Johnson formality. "Madame," he said, gesturing to the parents, "your children are slobs." After a moment of stunned silence, the parents broke into laughter and applause of agreement.

Perhaps a little embarrassed by his short tenure, Giamatti asked that his photograph not be hung on the wall with those of other masters. His request was honored, but instead the students affectionately hung a moose head over a polished brass plaque that reads "A. Bartlett Giamatti Memorial Moose." It remains in the college today.

During the three years before he became Yale's president, Giamatti served as director of the Division of the Humanities, one of the three bodies in the Faculty of Arts and Sciences (the Division of Social Sciences and the Division of the Sciences are the others) with general oversight over the departments and faculty. This assignment gave him a broad understanding of academic issues. He also undertook committee assignments, perhaps the most important of which was service on a committee appointed by Hanna Gray in 1977 to consider reform of Yale's finances.

But above all, Giamatti was a distinctive personality on the Yale campus, a blend of the actor's art and the verbal facility of the scholar and teacher. We have seen that he was a performer from childhood. Then he did impersonations. At Andover, he had taken on the pose of the world-weary cynic. Alvin Kernan has described the undergraduate Giamatti as "a very cool fellow, popular, exchanging easy jokes with anyone and everyone—'Hey, paisano!'" A friend of his from undergraduate days, back in New Haven after a couple of years studying abroad, remembers encountering him on the street, hunched over in a threadbare tweed coat, hands in pockets, a cigarette dangling from his lips. There was no standard greeting from an old friend when they passed, only a confidential whisper: "Blake's in. Donne's out."

Now a seasoned faculty member, he had become the consummate actor. A perceptive reporter for the *Yale Daily News* described him shortly before he became president of the university, holding court in the nave of Yale's gothic Sterling Library:

> Standing stooped like a Confucian scholar out of an old Chinese painting, swinging his old tan briefcase and looking straight ahead, he acknowledges the greetings of passing students and professors, says hello to a few who stop to listen. His subject is the need to cut the budget, and Giamatti is being typically quick and to the point, without the ponderous caution of many of his colleagues. He speaks in complete clear sentences, with few ums and ahs and false starts. His voice is a little thin and a little gravelly, but used to great

effect, the tone and pitch constantly varied like an actor's. Every few phrases he repeats some key word or phrase with high-pitched emphasis. "Seven million dollars in reductions in the next few years. SEVEN MILLION DOLLARS. It's incredible." . . . Along with the urban ethnic accent associated with a lot of good comedians, he has their perfect sense of timing. The faculty is "the faculty of Yale College assembled in solemn conclave." Yale is "this august institution. . . . " Standing before the stone arches of the card catalogue, with his goatee and the dark rings under his eyes and the circle of listeners gathered around him, he looks like he's been cast as an Elizabethan conspirator.

And his verbal facility had grown with the actor's timing. "Sometimes I thought of him as a glass blower," Maynard Mack has said. "He could blow iridescent creatures out of his mouth, turn them over and consider them. . . . Then, he would put them on the table and pull the cloth out from under them, and gaily, watch them go tinkling on the floor." At lunch one day, a companion of Giamatti's Yale classmate and friend John Wilkinson, secretary of the university during his presidency, expressed regret that he had never known Giamatti. "If he were sitting here," Wilkinson said, "you'd be mesmerized."

Scholar

Giamatti's principal interest as a teacher and scholar centered on the sixteenth-century poet of the English Renaissance Edmund Spenser, particularly his extended epic romance, *The Faerie Queene*. During most of the twentieth century—certainly throughout Giamatti's career—Spenser was seldom read and distinctly out of fashion. The century's most influential critic, T. S. Eliot, expressed the consensus when in 1931 he asked, "who, except scholars, and except the eccentric few who are born with a sympathy for such work . . . can now read through the whole of *The Faerie Queene* with delight?" Giamatti was sometimes teased about what others regarded as his esoteric literary interest. At a testimonial dinner for him shortly after he became president of Yale, the great Yale scholar of Italian language and literature Thomas Bergin, who taught both Giamatti and his father, needled him with his customary flair: "Lest the appreciation of our young prince carry us into unreserved adulation unworthy of honest men, we are constrained to look for some imperfections in him, and, of course, Bart is not without them. I have often reproached him for his misplaced esteem for the tedious and long-winded Spenser." Perhaps, Bergin concluded, it is "an indication of fortitude, however perverse."

But Giamatti came by his interest in Spenser naturally, for *The Faerie Queene* is directly descended from the Italian epic romances of the fifteenth and sixteenth centuries—Boiardo's *Orlando Innamorato*, Tasso's *Gerusalemme Liberata*, and above all, the *Orlando Furioso* of Ludovico Ariosto, from which many of the characters and episodes of *The Faerie Queene* are derived. "'Influence' is too weak a word," the great English critic C. S. Lewis has written, "for the relation which exists between the Italian epic and *The Faerie Queene*. To fight in another man's armour is something more than to be influenced by his style of fighting. Spenser is not merely helped by the Italians: the very kind to which his poem belongs was invented by them." Giamatti, steeped through his father and his studies at Yale in the literature of Italy, knew these poems, and the interest in Spenser inevitably followed.

The relationship between the Italian poets and Spenser is apparent in Giamatti's first book, a reworking of his Yale doctoral dissertation, published in 1966 as *The Earthly Paradise and the Renaissance Epic*. "The place of perfect repose and inner harmony," Giamatti writes, the desire for which has forever haunted mankind, "is always remembered as a garden." His book traces the development of the garden as such a symbol from the beginnings of Western literature through Milton. It begins with the myth of the Golden Age in ancient times, the Elysian Fields of the epics of Homer and Virgil, where all existence is a "dream of ease," with perfect climate, perpetual springtime, a sweet west wind, fruitful earth, shade, and water; and the settings and descriptions of the Greek and Roman pastoral poets and poets of nature. Next comes the medieval garden of courtly love, the setting for the French *Romance of the*

Rose, for the poems of the later French court poets, and, memorably, for the early poems of Chaucer. By the age of the Italian epics and *The Faerie Queene,* the love garden has become the realm of evil enchantresses, in the tradition of Homer's Circe, to which heroes are lured by a false illusion of beauty to their emasculation and ruin. And finally, in Milton's *Paradise Lost,* the Fall of Man in the Garden of Eden is reenacted.

As this summary suggests, Giamatti's book is a work of impressive range for so young a scholar. He reveals a close familiarity with Homer, Hesiod, and Pindar among the Greek poets, with Virgil, Ovid, Horace, Juvenal, Claudian, and Statius among the Romans, with the Italians Dante, Petrarch, Poliziano, Mantuan, and Trissino, as well as Boiardo, Tasso, and Ariosto, and with the *The Lusiads* of the Portuguese poet Camoens, an epic based on the voyage of Vasco da Gama to India and back. He deals with all of this poetry except the Greek in its original language. And of course the work contains extensive analyses of the poetry of Spenser and Milton.

Giamatti's first book established his reputation as a promising Renaissance scholar. It was widely and generally favorably reviewed, most importantly by the British scholar Frances Yates in the influential *New York Review of Books.* Giamatti, she wrote, "is a subtle psychologist, extremely sensitive to poetry—with the great advantage of being equally at home in Latin, Italian and English poetry. . . . This is comparative literature as it ought to be done, not the superficial tracing of 'sources,' but the organic study of a theme at a deep level."

Of particular interest in the book are the parallel treatments of the enchanted gardens of the Renaissance, for in considering Acrasia's Bower of Bliss in *The Faerie Queene* in relation to the two Italian gardens on which it is based, Ariosto's Garden of Alcina and Armida's garden in Tasso's work, Giamatti provides an important illustration of the influence of the Italian epic on Spenser.

"The classic Renaissance garden," he writes, "presents what poets from Ariosto to Spenser will expand—the beautiful paradise . . . where man's will is softened, his moral fiber unraveled, and his soul ensnared." This definition is certainly broad enough to encompass the gardens of both Ariosto and Tasso, but the emphasis is different in each. In Ariosto's garden, it is upon deception. Alcina is an illusionist, whose magic consists of her capacity to manipulate her environment so as to annihilate the distinction between appearance and reality. Here is the quintessential expression of the theme that so preoccupied the writers of the Renaissance, including Shakespeare, whose plays are full of disguises and misconceptions: the difficulty in distinguishing between what is and what seems to be. It can certainly be said of Ariosto's heroes who are Alcina's victims that their will is softened, their moral fiber unraveled, but only temporarily. They escape from Alcina the wiser for what has been essentially a learning experience.

Tasso's *Gerusalemme Liberata* followed Ariosto's *Orlando Furioso* at a distance of nearly half a century. The Counter-Reformation had intervened, and, as Giamatti points out, it was no longer possible for an Italian poet to write, as Ariosto had done, a poem largely without Christian content. In Tasso's work, the City of Jerusalem, whose recapture from the infidel is the poem's subject, is established as the center of Christian values and duty, to which Armida's garden stands in contrast as the place where duty is evaded for the sake of physical gratification. Armida is a sorceress like Alcina, but the emphasis is not on her art as deception, but rather on its effect on the souls of her victims. This is the dominant theme that carries over into Acrasia's Bower of Bliss in Spenser's poem. Acrasia's garden is the triumph of Art over Nature. It is

goodly beautifide
With all the ornaments of Floraes pride,
Wherewith her mother Art, as halfe in scorn
Of niggard Nature like a pompous bride
Did decke her, and too lavishly adorne.

It is thus counterfeit Nature, artificial, "unnatural," where a life of self-indulgence detains men from the pursuit of honor. Its victims do not escape better able to distinguish appearance from reality. They are transformed by Acrasia into beasts, forms symbolic of their degradation. Guyon, Spenser's Knight of Temperance in book II of *The Faerie Queene,* does not visit the Bower of Bliss as a learner or a victim, but as an avenger, who succeeds in his quest to destroy it.

All of this emerges from the excellent relevant chapters in Giamatti's book, but there is another garden that has greater significance for him and his career, a symbolic place of inner harmony that was for him a living ideal. It is best expressed as the earthly paradise of Dante, the vision of Eden before the Fall that comes in *The Divine Comedy* at the end of the second section, *Purgatory.* Here Virgil, traditionally seen as the personification of Reason, having guided Dante the pilgrim through the process of purgation, gives way to Beatrice, the personification of Faith. This garden is not the City of God, which Dante has not yet reached, but its earthly replica. It is, Giamatti writes, a place of "freedom within order [that] emphasizes the responsibility of a man, in his essential uniqueness, to conduct himself." It is, as we shall see, the ideal university that Giamatti describes in his collection of speeches entitled *A Free and Ordered Space.* It is baseball, "its freedom, structure and beauty," as he says in his book on the game entitled *Take Time for Paradise.*

Dante's earthly paradise represents an exception to the customary use of the garden in Western literature, at least after the myth of the Golden Age in the ancient world. Typically, proceeding from the biblical story of the temptation of Eve in the Garden of Eden, the garden, though beautiful, is a place of deception and danger. We have seen this use of it in the enchanted gardens of the Renaissance epic. We find similar uses both earlier and later. In the gardens of the medieval poetry of courtly love, we meet the allegorical figures that threaten the lover as he pursues his lady—Doubt, Daunger, Despight, Dissemblance, Fear, Jealousie, and the rest. Chaucer makes repeated use of the garden as a place of danger as well as beauty, placing many key episodes there in *The Canterbury Tales,* typically on a May morning. In "The Knight's Tale," the Theban knights Palamon and Arcite first observe Emelye from their prison window in a garden on "a morwe of May," both falling in love with her, causing the rupture in their friendship on which the whole tale turns. In a like setting Dorigen, the faithful wife of Arverigus, makes her fateful bargain with Aurelius in "The Franklin's Tale" to grant him her love if he can remove the rocks from the Brittany coast. And again, in "The Merchant's Tale," it is on a May morning, when "the turtles voys is herd" and "wynter is goon with alle his reynes weete," that the old lecher January, newly married to the young and nubile May, is cuckolded in his garden by Damyan. And so it is with Shakespeare, whose plays abound with garden settings, primarily in the comedies, but not exclusively. Hamlet's father is poisoned while "sleeping in my orchard." Indeed, for Hamlet himself the whole world is

> an unweeded garden
> That grows to seed; things rank and gross in nature
> Possess it merely.

When Giamatti chose the earthly paradise of Dante as the place of "freedom within order" to which all human institutions should aspire, he knew that departures from the ideal were a common literary theme. Giamatti admired Ariosto, whose *Orlando Furioso* in the then-standard English verse translation by William Stewart Rose he coedited in 1968, above all Italian poets after Dante. In Ariosto's poem, things are never what they seem. Ariosto, Giamatti writes, always confronts this reality in a spirit of tolerance that "reveals itself in a mingling of acceptance and regret; acceptance of the fact that nothing on earth can be regarded as fixed or finished or, finally, even true; and regret at the loss of codes of behavior which seemed to deal with the complexities of man's existence." For Giamatti himself, this spirit of tolerance and acceptance was sometimes hard to achieve when the institutions with which he was most concerned—the university and the world of baseball—failed to live up to the ideal of the earthly paradise. He possessed a strong streak of the moralist and idealist, and such failures often threatened to lead him into disillusion and resentment.

Giamatti's second book, *Play of Double Senses*, which he published in 1975, deals exclusively with *The Faerie Queene*. He writes in the preface that it is intended for students of Spenser, and it has the feel of an introduction. Only about 130 pages long, it contains several brief chapters providing background for Spenser's poem, including a summary of the poet's life, background on continental and English literary sources, a history of the myth of King Arthur (a central figure in the poem), and some commentary on the structure and principal themes of the work. All of this is largely unremarkable, though useful and interesting, and one is tempted to pass on without further comment to Giamatti's last and richest volume of criticism. But two chapters deserve some attention: one because it establishes a theme—in this case the quest—which, like the garden, resonates in Giamatti's writing on other issues; and the other, on the place of pageantry in Spenser's poem, because it demonstrates the imaginative impulse and sensitivity to verbal nuance—to etymology—that inform so much of Giamatti's scholarly work.

In the first of these chapters, "The Forms of Epic," Giamatti refers to the "old idea of the epic as a quest, a seeking in the world"—to destroy Troy and repossess Helen in *The Iliad*; to see the face of God in *The Divine Comedy*; or, in *The Faerie Queene*, to rescue Una's parents from the dragon in book I or to destroy Acrasia's Bower of Bliss in book II. But from another perspective, he says, the epic is often about getting home, returning from exile: exile from Ithaca and Penelope in *The Odyssey*; exile from Beatrice in Dante's poem; exile from the court of the Faery Queene in Spenser's. We shall see that the notion of the epic as a return from exile becomes for Giamatti a metaphor in other contexts, notably baseball, where it expresses the circularity of the game that is its essence.

In the second of the two chapters, "Pageant, Show, and Verse," we see an early example of the characteristic concern in Giamatti's criticism for etymology, here employed to illuminate various aspects of *The Faerie Queene* through analysis of multiple significances of a single term, *pageant*. Derived from the Middle English word *pagyn* and its contemporary Anglo-Latin synonym *pagina*, it had, Giamatti says, several meanings, among them (1) a scene acted on a stage, (2) a deceit or trick, an empty show without substance or reality, and (3, perhaps its most familiar modern meaning), an allegorical tableau exhibited, usually in a public setting, on a platform or stage. He shows how Spenser made use of all of them.

Giamatti explores the first of the three meanings—a scene acted on a stage—in its application to poetic narrative. He points out that the Anglo-Latin root of pageant—*pagina*—is the root of the English word *page*, and he observes that one can "write" a pageant because pageantry is a language, a way of talking about private concerns in a public manner, and thus akin to allegory, a way of talking about substance by way of surfaces. In this sense it may be used to refer to an episode within a book: in book III, where love is examined in a variety of facets from episode to episode as through a prism, the poet muses:

Wonder it is to see in diverse mindes
How diversly Love doth his pageaunts play,
And shewes his powre in variable kindes.

Or *pageant* can refer to an entire book: in his brief appearance early in book II, Redcrosse, the hero of book I, addresses Guyon, the hero of book II, as the knight "whose pageant next ensewes." And finally, to the poem as a whole. Giamatti quotes from one of the dedicatory sonnets to *The Faerie Queene*, in which the poet writes that "th'old heroes, . . . / In this same pageaunt have a worthy place," and concludes, "It is the epic that is the great pageant, . . . a spectacle of the various moods and modes of a man's life in the theater of the world."

The meaning of pageant as a deceit or trick, an empty show without substance or reality, becomes a means of dramatizing that most pervasive of the themes of *The Faerie Queene*, as of so much other Renaissance literature: the elusive task of distinguishing between appearance and reality, between what is and what seems to be. "We must school ourselves," Giamatti writes, "to recognize the difference between a surface, a pageant, or a word that celebrates something real, and a surface, a show, or a word that only hides a deceptive or empty core." He offers as an example an episode early in book II. Guyon comes upon a maid, beautiful but disheveled, whose squire tells him that she has been abused by a knight answering the description of Redcrosse, and urges him to exact retribution. But they are not what they seem. She is the corrupt Duessa and he is the wicked magician Archimago, two figures of evil ubiquitous in the poem.

> Her purpose was not such as she did faine,
> Ne yet her person such as it was seene;
> But under simple shew and semblant plaine
> Lurkt false Duessa, secretly unseene,
> As a chaste virgin, that had wronged been;
> So had false Archimago her disguysed. . . .
> And eke himselfe had craftily devised
> To be her squire.

Here are words of pageantry—*shew* (show) and *semblant* (semblance)—used to denote deceit.

To illustrate Spenser's use of pageant in its third sense—as an allegorical tableau—Spenser reaches outside the poem to import context that explains and enriches its meaning. He draws upon the Elizabethan reader's familiarity with a public pageant embodying a myth central to the poem: that Elizabeth was the rightful successor of King Arthur because the rise of the royal House of Tudor in the person of her grandfather Henry VII represented the fulfillment of the traditional prophecy of Merlin that Arthur would return again to rule Britain. In this pageant the Lady of the Lake appears to the queen. She is the figure who in Arthurian myth gave Arthur his sword Excalibur, the surrender of which, after his last battle, to the lake from which it came is associated with his journey to the faery isle of Avalon to recover from his wounds. She explains, in a series of poetic stanzas, that she has returned from "a life in restless paine" occasioned by the successive control of Britain by the Saxons, the Danes, and the Normans, brought back by the "happy hope" of the accession of the Tudors. Henry VII regarded his own accession as the return of Arthur; he burnished the myth by calling his first son Arthur, and Britain would have had a king of that name had the boy not died before his father. In the pageant, the Lady of the Lake is represented as appearing first to Elizabeth, the third of the Tudor line, rather than to Henry. This suggestion that the queen's accession occasions the return of Arthur is adopted by Spenser in *The Faerie Queene*. Arthur appears repeatedly in the poem in the course of his quest to seek out and wed the Faery Queene, Spenser's personification of the sovereign herself.

In 1984 Yale University Press published, as *Exile and Change in Renaissance Literature*, a collection of seven essays by Giamatti that had appeared in various publications between 1968 and 1982. They were written, Giamatti says in his preface, in furtherance of a project to study the impact of the Italian Renaissance on the English Renaissance, a project to which he was urged to return at the end of his Yale presidency by colleagues who hoped he would rejoin the Yale faculty. They represent some of his best scholarly work, demonstrating the range, imagination, and sensitivity to etymology and language we have already observed.

Those qualities are memorably illustrated in the essay written last, "Hippolytus Among the Exiles: The Romance of Early Humanism," which appeared in 1982 in a collection of essays in honor of Giamatti's Yale colleague Louis L. Martz. The essay concerns itself with the sense of exile from the values of the ancient world that animated the men of the Renaissance, and their attempts to return from that exile through the restoration of ancient texts first known only in fragments. The title of the essay recalls the story, told in book VII of Virgil's *Aeneid*, of Hippolytus—torn to pieces by wild horses at the direction of his father, Theseus, on the basis of a false accusation of improper advances by his stepmother Phaedra, whose illicit love Hippolytus has spurned—and his restoration to life by the medicines of Aesculapius. The story provides a metaphor for the restoration by the Renaissance of fragmentary ancient texts.

Giamatti tells of the restoration of the text of the *Institutes* of the first-century Roman rhetorician Quintilian. In 1350, more than a half-century before the recovery of the full text, Petrarch was presented with an incomplete manuscript. He took the occasion to compose a "letter" to Quintilian, in which he says that the work has come into his hands, but only in a mutilated form. *Discerptus* is Petrarch's Latin adjective (from *discerpere*, to mutilate), a term also used by Virgil in the *Fourth Georgic* to describe Orpheus torn apart by the Thracian wives. The full text was discovered in the tower of a German monastery by an Italian bibliophile in 1419. The story is put forth as an example of the process of the recovery of ancient texts, and the symbolic return from exile that it represents.

Giamatti writes of "the etymologizing habit, the philological cast of mind, . . . typical of the whole humanist effort to uncover and reconstitute meaning by returning to origins." And he gives an example that reveals it as his own habit and cast of mind as well. He translates from Giovanni Boccaccio's *Genealogia Deorum Gentilium* (Genealogy of the Gods), the encyclopedic work on myth drawing from ancient treatises and writers that occupied the last thirty years of his life. Boccaccio writes of his labors to collect the scattered writings of the ancient authors, "torn limb from limb [*membratim discerptum:* Petrarch's word, Virgil's word] and scattered among the rough and desert places of antiquity; . . . [and] fit them together, like another Aesculapius restoring Hippolytus." Giamatti seems almost gleeful in pointing out, in his bracketed insert within the translation, the echo of past use in Boccaccio's text.

There is some other scholarly work to Giamatti's credit—a few miscellaneous essays, some translations, three volumes of literary texts under his general editorship entitled *Western Lit-*

erature (in which Spenser is, surprisingly, represented by only a single sonnet), a collection of essays on Dante edited by him entitled *Dante in America*. But these three books, *The Earthly Paradise and the Renaissance Epic*, *Play of Double Senses*, and *Exile and Change in Renaissance Literature*, represent the heart of his scholarly accomplishment. A senior Yale colleague of Giamatti, and a great admirer, asked informally to evaluate the quality of his work, pronounced it "good," then, after a pause, added "imaginative." Imagination may be the salient quality of his writings, but it is grounded in wide reading and sound scholarship. He was not a great scholar—there was no unique contribution to the understanding of his age or his field of concentration. But when he left the world of scholarship behind for the Yale presidency, though barely forty years old, his academic reputation rested on a solid base of achievement.

Teacher

In a corner of the Old Campus at Yale there is a tangible memorial to Giamatti. It is an unadorned black granite bench, on which are inscribed his own words: "A liberal education is at the heart of a civil society, and at the heart of a liberal education is the act of teaching." It is appropriate that these words should have been chosen, for as a teacher in the college classroom Giamatti was a supreme artist.

To Giamatti teaching was not simply the imparting of information. But neither was it haphazard discussion. Rather it was a carefully controlled process by which the student is encouraged to grow. Giamatti described the process in a talk entitled "A Liberal Education in a Civil Society" that he delivered several times during his presidency to groups of Yale alumni:

> The teacher's power and responsibility lies in choosing where everyone will begin and how, from that beginning, the end will be shaped. The choice of the final form lies in the teacher's initial act. . . . No good teacher ever wants to control the contour of another mind. That would not be teaching, it would be some form of terrorism. But no good teacher wants the contour of another mind to be ungainly, haphazard, randomly

energetic. Somehow the line between encouraging a design, and imposing a specific stamp, must be found, and abided, and clarified. . . .

Teaching is an instinctual art, . . . where one rehearses constantly while acting, sits as a spectator at a play one directs, engages every part in order to keep the choices open and the shape alive for the student, so that the student may enter in and begin to do what the teacher has chosen to begin: make choices. . . . [In good teaching] you feel what you think, embody what you say, do what you talk about—judge as you talk about judgment, proceed logically as you reveal logical structure, clarify as you talk about clarity . . . —all in the service of encouraging the student in imitation and then repetition of the process you have been summoning, all so that he may turn himself not into you but into himself.

The process begins by establishing the relationship between teacher and student. Giamatti, unlike most of his colleagues, who preferred teaching in seminar style around a large table, always chose for his freshman English classes the old-fashioned classroom with chairs bolted to the floor in rows facing the teacher standing in the front behind a lectern. Any implication of equality between teacher and student was thus discouraged. But if the primacy of the master was established, so was the respect that he owes to his students. Giamatti always called them by their last names—Miss Jones or Mr. Smith. "I call you by your last names, because you call me by my last name—to show an equivalent amount of respect between teacher and student," he told his freshmen. But there were limits. One year a freshman named Scott Cantor suggested that the same equivalency could be achieved if Giamatti called students by their first names and they called him Bart. "A slow smile came to the bearded professor," Cantor recalls, "but the tone of the last two words of his response came out quite serious: 'That's not my style—Mr. Cantor.'"

Notwithstanding this environment of formality, Giamatti's classes were always lively. His strong theatrical bent and ready wit were constantly on display. "The class was so full of personality, and, to use Chaucer's expression, 'fellowship,'" one student recalls. "To this day I can list almost every member of that class—something I can't say for any other class in my years at Yale. . . . It was like being a member of a secret club. . . . There was always passion in his teaching, always humor. . . . He loved teaching, his students, and our ideas, and we loved him back." A student in his course on *The Faerie Queene* remembers that "there was a breeziness, an easiness, a lightness—and a sly leprechaun-ish quality—about Professor Giamatti's approach to Spenser's epic. . . . He projected the sense . . . that he had found his special patented easy way through the thicket of these immensely dense cantos, and we just needed to stick close to him and we wouldn't get too badly scratched by the underbrush."

But for all the good fellowship and humor, there was rigor. The Socratic method of give and take employed by Giamatti was not for sissies; he could be brusque, even adversarial and sarcastic, but a bright beam of warmth in the end shone through. Giamatti liked to teach freshmen and sophomores. It was essential, he thought, for students to learn early in their college careers the centrality of language to Western culture and, therefore, the importance of close attention to texts. By junior year, he told his students, it was already too late. He made a powerful impression that affected their whole Yale experience. A few comments from former students will illustrate: "Mr. Giamatti's teaching was memorable." "His influence was strong." "I have many powerful impressions of him and his course." "It's hard to know where to start, or how to describe what a wonderful teacher he was." And it is astonishing how much so many still remember: "The themes I remember learning about were fellowship, the value of experience, the need to come home—themes that pertain to Chaucer's pilgrims, Spenser's knights, and baseball's shortstops and second basemen as well. He taught us how it all fit together." "The most abiding impressions of Spenser and *The Faerie Queene* that he imparted to me were: 1. Mutabilitie—nothing is what it seems. . . . Swords have two edges. And words can kill. Or heal. . . . 2. Futility—going on is all we know of poetry and possibly all we know of life. The pathetic impulse to create a poem [the unfinished *Faerie Queene*] that can never be completed."

Giamatti maintained a continuing interest—and often a continuing relationship—with his former students. A member of the freshman English course that Giamatti taught in the fall of 1977, his last before he became president of Yale, recalls that the class held a reunion with their professor each spring while they were undergraduates, the first three at the Old Heidelberg restaurant on Chapel Street, and the fourth at the President's House on Hillhouse Avenue. In May 1986, at their fifth Yale reunion, they met with him again, for lunch at Mory's, where they brought their old professor up to date on what they had been doing during the intervening five years and their plans for the future. Giamatti was near the end of his tenure as Yale's president, and when they asked him about his own future plans, he told them that he would either go back to teaching and research or do something "completely different and unusual." A month later it was announced that he had accepted an offer to become president of the National League.

Giamatti often formed a friendship and continuing relationship with Yale undergraduates who were not his students. While he was president of Yale, he advised freshmen during their orientation to find a professor they admired and invite him or her to lunch. Stacy Andersen of the Class of 1983 and her roommates invited Giamatti himself, in their freshman year and in each year thereafter. He always accepted. "It was a wonderful experience for us," she remembers, "and many of his words of wisdom have remained important to me in the years that followed. He was one of the world's gems."

The reader was introduced in an earlier chapter to Judith Sizer, the daughter of the headmaster of Andover, whom Giamatti persuaded to attend Yale rather than Harvard. The story of Giamatti's continuing place in her life illustrates the interest he regularly took in young people and the positive influence he often had on them. Sizer entered Yale as a freshman in 1977, the year in which Giamatti was chosen as president, and she was a sophomore when he took office. Her parents were his friends; he had been a trustee of Andover in the early years of Theodore Sizer's headmastership, and he was a frequent guest in the Sizer home when he attended meetings. It was therefore natural that she should stay in touch with him, and she occasionally dropped into his office to visit with him. In the spring of her junior year, she enrolled in a small seminar that Giamatti, Yale's president, gave with his close friend the great historian of religion Jaroslav Pelikan on Dante and Aquinas.

When Sizer graduated in 1981, she wanted a job at Yale to earn money for postgraduate education, and Giamatti went to bat for her, writing a letter on her behalf that resulted in her being hired by the office of the Yale Alumni Fund. Intermittent contact between the two continued. In the fall of 1983 Giamatti's administrative assistant went on maternity leave, and Sizer was asked to fill in for her on a temporary basis, retaining her position at the Alumni Fund and dividing her time between the two assignments. When the administrative assistant decided not to return, Sizer took over her job full-time. She served throughout the 1983–84 academic year, acting as what she calls Giamatti's "paper person," performing the customary tasks of an administrative assistant: screening his mail, drafting routine letters for his signature, gathering and organizing materials for meetings. In the fall of 1984 she left to enter Harvard Law School, graduating in 1987 to begin a legal career that has led to her current place in the world of education as general counsel at Brandeis University. Sizer remained in touch with Giamatti after she left Yale until his death in 1989. She says that she never stopped learning from him and that she still misses his advice whenever she has an important problem to face or decision to make.

The inscription on Giamatti's memorial bench at Yale tells us that teaching as an art does not exist in a vacuum but is "at the heart of a liberal education." We shall have occasion in a later chapter, when we examine the talks—described there as homilies—that he delivered to Yale students during his presidency, to learn in depth his view of the meaning and purpose of a liberal education. He taught that it is an ordering and broadening of the mind for the purpose of fostering participation in the good work of the world as a constructive citizen. It is a lesson he never ceased repeating. The lesson is contained in one of his final communications to Judith Sizer.

In 1988 he sent her a presentation copy of a collection of his speeches published that year, *A Free and Ordered Space: The Real World of the University.* He inscribed it as "The Wizened One." She knew immediately the source of the inscription, although it is omitted from the text of the speeches as they appear in the book. His baccalaureate address to graduating seniors in 1984, her last spring as his administrative assistant, entitled "Give Time to Time," was preceded by what Giamatti calls a "fable," in which a figure identified only as "the wizened one," who lives in "a village not far from the sea where spring had finally come," calls together a group of wise councillors to advise on an appropriate subject for a baccalaureate speech.

"There then ensued," Giamatti says, "the sound of wisdom being offered, which was a deep and velvety silence." He finally accepts the advice of the youngest councillor to speak about time and how the students must live in time.

The wizened one takes as his text a rabbinical aphorism of the second century—"You are not required to complete the work, but neither are you free to desist from it"—which Giamatti's friend and colleague Harold Bloom has glossed as follows: "The work cannot be completed in time, yet we must work as if there will be time to complete it, 'to give time to time,' as in the Sephardic proverb." Giamatti observes that "late in the day of a century or a millennium the culture always feels itself in decline," and a kind of fatigue accumulates that can stifle creative effort and lead to the acceptance of dangerous easy answers. He urges the students not to succumb to this "sense of enervation and anxiety" but instead to engage actively in the good work of the world, "to give time to time"— to use their liberal education, that is, for its true civic purpose. At the end of the talk, the fable resumes:

> There the speaker ended, and now our fable, with which we began, almost ends. Save to say that it was now dark in the village not far from the sea. As the councillors silently scattered into the night, they could see the lights that had been lit all over the village. The villagers were wise in their own way: they knew that they best face the dark by lighting the lights in their houses. The villagers knew that it always gets late, and that when it does, the truly wise will make a light and use the time.

President-Designate

In December 1976 the newly elected President of the United States, Jimmy Carter, named as his Secretary of State Cyrus R. Vance, a member of the Yale Corporation and a close friend of President Brewster. The following March it became known that Carter intended to appoint Brewster as ambassador to Great Britain. The appointment was officially announced in early April, and Brewster submitted his resignation as Yale's president, to take effect after commencement in May. Under Yale's bylaws, Hanna Gray, the provost, became acting president until Brewster's successor took office.

Simultaneously with the announcement of Brewster's resignation, the Yale Corporation appointed seven of its members as a committee, under the chairmanship of William P. Bundy, to coordinate the search for a new president. Giamatti was among those at Yale mentioned as a possible candidate in the initial speculation, but the tentative criteria privately developed by the committee would have excluded him. Yale's financial difficulties dictated, the committee believed, a person with managerial experience, which Giamatti lacked. Moreover, it was thought that Yale would benefit from the perspective of a person familiar with other universities; this led to a predisposition to look outside of Yale for Brewster's successor. One or two university presidents meeting these criteria might have had the Yale job had they not expressed the desire to stay where they were. As for Giamatti himself, he disclaimed any knowledge of his possible status as a candidate. "It's news to me," he said. "The only thing I ever wanted to be president of was the American League."

The search proceeded throughout the spring and summer and into the fall. Dozens of potential candidates were vetted, often through interviews of associates or other persons familiar with their qualifications. One such person was the economist Henry Rosovsky, dean of the Faculty of Arts and Sciences at Harvard, who was interviewed by committee member Lance M. Liebman, then a young faculty member at the Harvard Law School, now a professor and former dean at the Columbia Law School. The principal purpose of the interview was to solicit Rosovsky's views as to possible candidates within the Harvard community, but his observations were so astute, and his grasp of educational issues so assured, that Liebman saw at once that Rosovsky himself was fully qualified to lead Yale. Inquiries by committee members of Rosovsky's Harvard colleagues validated that conclusion, and he soon became a leading candidate.

The process drew to its conclusion when Rosovsky and two others were brought to Washington on December 6 to be interviewed by the full membership of the Yale Corporation. Rosovsky was reluctant to come. He had made it plain to the search committee, and he now reiterated, that he was not at all sure he would accept the Yale presidency even if offered. He understood the honor it conferred and the challenge it presented, but he had no ties to Yale—his undergraduate degree was from William and Mary and his Ph.D. from Harvard. He had a deep affection for Harvard, where he had spent most of his professional career. He was urged to come anyway. And at the end of the interviews, it was decided to offer him the presidency of Yale, despite the risk of embarrassment to the university if the offer should become known and he should refuse it. Perhaps the members of the Corporation, men and women of Yale, could not quite believe that the presidency of their university, once in fact offered, would be turned down.

A small delegation of Corporation members flew the same afternoon to Boston to convey the offer in person. Rosovsky asked for time to think it over and for access to all available data on Yale's budgetary problems. Henry Broude, a Yale economist then serving as special assistant to the university president, and a friend of Rosovsky's from graduate school days at Harvard, was sent to Cambridge to provide it. The two men spent a weekend reviewing the data. There was more soul searching. But early in the week of December 15, Rosovsky advised the Corporation that he did not wish to leave Harvard. It was not, he told them, the budgetary problems that prompted his decision; they were certainly manageable. It was that he lacked the emotional commitment to Yale he thought necessary to do a first-rate job. Unfortunately, during the period that Rosovsky was considering the offer, word of it leaked out. There are conflicting versions of how this happened. One has it that a reporter on a transatlantic flight overheard a Corporation member discussing the offer with his wife; another, perhaps more likely, says that a Harvard faculty member, in Moscow to attend a conference and dining at the U.S. embassy, talked loosely at dinner, unaware that one of the other guests was the Moscow bureau chief for a prominent American newspaper. No one suggests that the leak was deliberate. But however it occurred, when Rosovsky withdrew, Yale was embarrassed, and some members of the Yale community, unaware of the facts, unfairly blamed him.

Rosovsky's withdrawal left the Yale Corporation in a difficult position. They had no obvious alternative candidate. The two other men who had been interviewed in Washington were not thought right for the job. The only other promising name was Giamatti's, who had earlier emerged as the leading candidate among Yale insiders, but he had not even been interviewed. Should he be considered, even though he failed to meet the criteria—managerial experience and outside affiliation—on which the search had proceeded? Or should the search be reopened? The latter course raised the question of who would lead Yale while the reopened search was in progress, for by this time Hanna Gray had accepted the presidency of the University of Chicago and would be leaving at the end of the academic year. At this juncture the senior fellow of the Corporation, J. Richardson Dilworth, who had stayed in the background during the search, stepped forward with the strong recommendation that a choice should be made promptly. The leadership vacuum during a reopened search would be intolerable, he said, and in any event there was no reason to believe that the potential candidates who had been found wanting since the spring would now seem acceptable. So it was decided to interview Giamatti, together with a late entry whose name had been put forward by a new member of the Corporation.

We have seen that Giamatti had been coy about his interest in the Yale presidency. He aspired, he had said, only to be president of the American League. But privately he desperately wanted the job. He had been beside himself with disappointment when he learned it had been offered to Rosovsky; his neighbor in the Hall of Graduate Studies remembers that he nearly dismantled his office in frustration when the news reached him. Now there had been an unexpected reprieve.

The interviews took place on Saturday, December 17, in a

frigid President's House on Hillhouse Avenue, vacant and un-
heated since the Brewsters had departed in the summer for
London. It was the perfect format for the articulate and charismatic Giamatti, and the following day the members of the
Corporation voted to offer him the Yale presidency. Members
of the search committee, including the two members of the
Corporation closest in age to Giamatti—his undergraduate
contemporary Liebman (Class of 1962) and Strobe Talbott
(Class of 1968)—went to his house in Westville to make the
offer. A day later, after the formality of talking it over with
family and friends, Giamatti accepted. The public announcement was made on Tuesday, December 20. Giamatti was thirty-
nine years old. He would be forty when he took office the
following July 1, the youngest president of Yale since the eigh-
teenth century.

His appointment was generally greeted with glee on the
Yale campus, where he was a popular figure with both colleagues and students. "A human being as president of a university—my God, what will that be like?" said his friend Donald
Kagan. "We're going to be laughing in the aisles, he'll be so
good." The wit and informality so many admired in him were in
evidence in an interview he gave to the education editor of the
New York Times shortly after his appointment. He was asked
about his earlier remark that the only thing he ever wanted to
be president of was the American League. Did that mean Yale
was his second choice? "I wouldn't say second choice," he
replied. "I said that about the American League about four
months ago and figured that I would sit back and see if there
was any movement. The baseball meetings came and went, and
the big trades took place, and nothing happened—no phone
calls from the Commissioner. Then I did get this extraordinarily
gracious call from the Yale Corporation, so I thought: Well, you
do what you have to do."

Giamatti's appointment was to be effective on July 1, 1978. Hanna Gray would continue as president (she had been given the title during her year in charge) until that date. In the meantime Giamatti would concentrate on issues of long-range planning, educating himself by consulting with alumni, colleagues, and others in New Haven and across the country. He would mostly listen. "Right now," he would tell an interviewer in March, "I'm the Aeolian harp of Woodbridge Hall. The impulses of the vernal woods sing right through me."

This interval offers an opportunity to assess the qualities that the new president would bring to his job.

First, of course, he was widely respected and trusted by his faculty colleagues. This would be particularly important when it came to the cost-cutting measures that Yale's budgetary problems would inevitably require; it would be easier for the faculty to take the medicine from one of its own than from an outsider.

Giamatti, known to be culturally and politically conservative (at least for a college professor), was also popular with alumni. It was no secret that Kingman Brewster had forfeited considerable support among graduates by instituting a new admissions policy that sharply reduced the number of sons of alumni admitted to the college and brought women to Yale, and by his opposition to the war in Vietnam and his handling of the May Day crisis. Too liberal, many alumni thought. The consequences of this erosion of support could be most dramatically seen in the troubles of the Campaign for Yale, the $370 million capital drive launched in the spring of 1974 and scheduled to be completed by the end of 1977. At the beginning of the final year, the campaign had raised less than half of its goal. Brewster knew that his unpopularity among conservative alumni was impeding its success. Perhaps a hundred million dollars could be raised, he ruefully suggested, by auctioning off his resignation. In the final event, after an eighteen-month extension, the goal was reached, half of it raised in the two fiscal years after Brewster's resignation, including more than $100 million in the first year of Giamatti's presidency.

Giamatti would bring to the presidency a wide familiarity with how Yale operated and the issues facing it. He had been the master of a college—for a short time to be sure, but long enough to understand and appreciate the role of the colleges in Yale life. He had been director of the Division of Humanities, one of the three divisions into which the Faculty of Arts and Sciences was divided for the purpose of overseeing the departments and faculty in Yale College. And at the time of his election, he was serving on an important committee appointed by Hanna Gray to develop a program to bring Yale's finances into equilibrium. ·

Together with a knowledge of how Yale worked, Giamatti would bring a deep emotional commitment to the institution. Except for the two years of "exile" in Princeton, Yale had been his home for more than twenty years. It was his father's school. It was his life. Henry Rosovsky had understood how important emotional commitment to the institution is for a university president; the absence of that feeling for Yale was the principal reason he had given for declining the offer of its presidency. Giamatti would labor under no such handicap.

Finally, Giamatti would bring to his new job a coherent vision of what a university should be, rooted in the values of the Renaissance, whose study had been his intellectual life; and the unmatched eloquence to set that vision forth. This he did in the speeches he gave each year to the incoming freshman class and the graduating senior class—"homilies," Maynard Mack called them. We shall be looking at them in some detail in a later chapter, for they are a defining legacy of his presidency.

Yet for all these virtues, Giamatti lacked the managerial experience the Yale Corporation had hoped for in the new president. He surely possessed some of the qualities essential to a good manager: a firm grasp of the issues facing his institution; a clarity of thought and expression free of the woolliness that is part of the prevailing caricature of the academic mind; a clear conviction of Yale's purpose. Untested, though, were the personal qualities that effective management also requires: the ability to delegate and to work productively with strong colleagues; and above all, the ability to mediate conflict and to handle stress. Scholarship and teaching are not inherently team sports, fostering the collaborative instinct and providing experience in resolving conflicts. It remained to be seen whether Giamatti possessed these qualities.

There were some disquieting signs. Bart had a thousand friends, it was said, all of whom imagined they were close to him when they were in his presence. His interest in them was genuine, but those who knew him best recognized that behind the variety of personae Giamatti the actor presented to the outside world, behind the bantering wit and the capacity for ready friendship, was an intensely private man. He was proud of his Italian heritage, but defensive if he thought it was slighted. He betrays this sensitivity in an introduction that he wrote to a book published in 1987 entitled *The Italian Americans,* in which he says, surely thinking of himself, that "any Italian-American who has achieved more prominence than many in the non-Italian American majority would have thought 'believable' or 'expected' can tell . . . of how patronizing otherwise sensible acquaintances suddenly become, of how often . . . comments will contain slighting . . . references to an Italian heritage." In the same introduction he calls the family "one of the sustaining ideals of the Italian American," and he suggests that it was for him a sanctuary from a sometimes hostile outside world, "where one does not have to be on guard, where one can assume support and nurture." In one of his books, dedicated to his wife, he identifies her with Una, the angelic heroine of book I of *The Faerie Queene,* who has "made a sunshine in the shady place." We have seen that few people had ever visited his home; he drew a clear line between his family and his professional life. Did this reliance on the family as a refuge imply a reluctance to rely on and delegate to others, an instinct for playing it close to the vest, even a secretiveness, that would inhibit Giamatti from recruiting and working with strong colleagues in collaborative relationships?

Some of his colleagues who knew Giamatti best and admired him most were aware of a second troublesome sign: his acute sensitivity and vulnerability to criticism. When the inevitable resentments and suspicions in a time of budget cutbacks descend upon him, his friend Donald Kagan observed, "he'll take it hard. He's not thick-skinned. He'll lick his wounds and come out all right, but it'll cost him. . . . He's a sensitive man." Maynard Mack pronounced him "tender as a glowworm." Giamatti himself seems to have been aware of his vulnerability. He knew he would be criticized, even vilified, for some of the actions he would have to take to restore Yale's financial health. "When I leave this job," he told friends, "I expect to be a cinder." Successful leaders learn to accept criticism philosophically as part of their job. Would Giamatti's sensitivity—growing out of his need for approval—make such acceptance difficult, leading him to internalize criticism and retreat into a defensive posture at times of stress that would cloud his judgment?

There was, too, the matter of Giamatti's health. He seemed supremely indifferent to his own physical well-being. As a scholar he was a workaholic, staying up late at his studies and postponing rest even further by watching a late movie. Often exhausted, he would become ill, occasionally requiring hospitalization. He developed kidney problems; in 1981 a kidney stone had to be removed. He suffered from Charcot-Marie-Tooth disease, a congenital muscular atrophying of the lower legs that affected some members of the Giamatti family. It is a progressive malady; Valentine Giamatti, who also suffered from it, walked with difficulty in the last years of his life. Its effects, including the strain it puts on the heart, can be alleviated by leg braces. Bart Giamatti would not wear them.

Giamatti was undisciplined in his habits. He indulged in rich foods, lunching on double cheeseburgers and frequently holding court on weekends in the local deli. There was candy in his office to pop into his mouth. As a result, the naturally slim young "prince" of the early years put on weight. And most destructive of all, he was addicted to nicotine all of his adult life, chain-smoking cigarettes during every waking hour. It was a particularly dangerous addiction for Giamatti, for the family history was not encouraging. His father, also a heavy smoker, suffered a serious heart attack in his early fifties that nearly killed him. He changed his lifestyle and lived another twenty years, though at a slower pace. When a similar attack struck his son, there was no second chance.

Overeating and heavy smoking are the common habits of people who have trouble handling stress. Many of Giamatti's friends tried without success to persuade him to live a healthier life—to diet, to reduce his dependence on cigarettes, to establish a regimen of exercise. It is a matter of speculation to what extent his lifestyle affected his performance as Yale's president; it seems safe to assume that he did not feel his best at all times. The fatal reckoning did not come until after he had left Yale.

Finally, Bart Giamatti carried into his presidency an identity for which he could be neither praised nor blamed: he was not Kingman Brewster. Their differences in background were, of course, obvious to all. Brewster was the quintessential New England Yankee aristocrat, an eleventh-generation lineal male descendant of Elder William Brewster, the spiritual head of the Mayflower and chief religious prefect of the Plymouth Colony. Giamatti was the grandson of a working-class Italian immigrant. Obvious, too, were their differences in style and outlook. Brewster was calm and assured. Giamatti was highstrung and sensitive to criticism. Brewster, though essentially moderate and pragmatic, had his cultural and political roots in a patrician tradition of independent progressivism. Giamatti was culturally deeply conservative.

There is little evidence that these differences affected the personal relations between the two men, which seem always to have been cordial. Giamatti went out of his way to praise to his friends the warm hospitality he had received from the Brewsters when he visited them in London shortly after his appointment as Brewster's successor. Brewster must have known that Giamatti was one of those faculty members who was unsympathetic with the student activism of the sixties and suspicious of Brewster's toleration of it, but unlike his friend Donald Kagan and others, he was not an open and conspicuous critic. There was, of course—as is to be expected when there is a change in the administration of any institution—some resentful grumbling among the loyalists of both men, but it was not enough to cause serious friction in the transition.

All of this calm reflected the fact that by 1978 the turmoil of the sixties, which so dramatically demonstrated the differences in style and outlook between Brewster and Giamatti, was in the receding past. When Giamatti took office, eight full academic years had passed since May Day and the end of the sixties at Yale. The bitter cultural differences of that era were, if not over, at least in abeyance. Brewster's Age of Camelot, as his close circle of admirers remembered it, had passed. Everyone knew it was time—many thought past time—for him to leave. He seemed bored, and he was frustrated by a set of financial problems he was not well equipped to deal with. The new administration was welcomed, and its leader entered office with every good wish for his success.

But the cultural and political divisions of the sixties did not permanently go away; they were fundamental, part of an historic tearing asunder of American sensibilities and consensus. They involved clashes in outlook as to what a university is for, where the responsibility for determining its policies should lie, how students and faculty should comport themselves in political and academic disputes. They reflected, with a ferocity only rarely present in the life of an institution and its political and cultural milieu, a confrontation between those who embraced traditional values and those who wished to see them replaced by something new. When late in the Giamatti administration disputes arose—between Yale and its white-collar workers over wages, and between its governing body and its students and faculty over investment policy—the emotions of the sixties flared up again, sometimes with all of the ideological fervor of the earlier time, and Giamatti found himself measured against the memory of his predecessor.

Giamatti assumed the presidency of Yale as scheduled on July 1, 1978. The formal inauguration ceremony, full of pomp and tradition, took place on the following October 14. After the procession of faculty members and representatives of other universities in colorful academic robes, the keys, charter, and seal of the university were presented to the new president. In his inaugural address Giamatti sounded many familiar themes: Yale must put its financial house in order, using its resources

prudently, imaginatively, and wisely; Yale must foster an atmosphere of mutual regard and collaboration with the city of New
Haven, with which its future is intertwined; Yale must expend
every effort to nourish and encourage its young faculty, for "the
faculty is at the heart of this place . . . and at the heart of the
faculty in a place like Yale is the teaching function." But the
theme that Giamatti first established is the one to which as
president he would return again and again: that a university is
in essence a place where freedom and order must coexist to
educate men and women for a civic function:

> A civilized order is the precondition of freedom, and freedom
> —of belief, speech and choice—the goal of responsible order.
> A university cannot expound those goals and expect a larger
> society to find them compelling, it cannot become a reposi-
> tory of national hope and a source of national leadership,
> unless it strives to practice what it teaches. . . .
>
> Intellectual and civic in nature, pluralistic in purpose and
> composition, hierarchical in structure, the University exists
> for that play of restraint and release in each of its individual
> members. . . .
>
> Thus it is so powerful and so fragile, the foe of the merely
> random, insistent on order while urging freedom, convinced
> that the human mind, out of nature, can fashion shapes and
> patterns nature never bore, and convinced that it is prime
> among the artifacts.

1. Bart Giamatti on the day of his inauguration as Yale president

2. Peggy Giamatti, Bart's mother, an important contributor to
the family's cultural life

3. Val Giamatti, Bart's father, conducting a seminar of Mount Holyoke under-graduates in his living room at South Hadley, Massachusetts

4. On sabbatical in Italy, 1948–49: Peggy and Val with their children (from left), Elria, Dino, and Bart

5. The 1954–55 sabbatical: Bart with Capri in the background

6. The Yale president with his father . . .

7. . . . . and with his mother

8. As a senior in Yale College

9. As a young member of the
Princeton faculty

10. Yale's new assistant professor with his wife, Toni . . .

11. . . . and in the classroom at Yale

12. The "prince" in his Yale office

13. Yale's president-elect with his wife, Toni, and his children (from left), Paul, Elena, and Marcus

14. President Giamatti with his immediate predecessors, Kingman
Brewster and Hanna Gray

15. In procession on inauguration day

16. The president speaking to alumni beneath the banner of Yale

17. With his friend Ben DiLieto, the mayor of New Haven, on
Communiversity Day

18. Leading the band on a football Saturday at the Yale Bowl

19. At Doubleday Field in Cooperstown, New York, home of the National Baseball Hall of Fame

20. Taking in a ballgame with Fay Vincent, his friend and successor as commissioner of baseball

21. A weary and saddened commissioner, in front of the logo of Major League Baseball, announcing the lifetime suspension of Pete Rose

22. The memorial bench on Yale's Old Campus: "A liberal education is at the heart of a civil society, and at the heart of a liberal education is the act of teaching"

Yale:
University President

Some Early
Personnel Decisions

Giamatti himself has famously described how his presidency of Yale began. He needed, he wrote, a policy. He had "a mortgage and one suit," but no policy. And then, one spring evening in 1978,

> crouched in my garage . . . it came to me, and I wrote, right there, between the lawnmower and the snow tires, a memo. On July 1, 1978, my first day in office, I issued this memo to an absent and indifferent University. It read
>
>> To the members of the University Community:
>> In order to repair what Milton called the ruin of our grand parents, I wish to announce that henceforth, as a matter of University policy, evil is abolished and paradise is restored.
>> I trust all of us will do whatever possible to achieve this policy objective.

Between the lines of Giamatti's lighthearted (and apocryphal) summary of the reactions to this pronouncement, we see aspects of the "evil" lingering from the Brewster years that the new administration would need to confront. An alumnus in New York, Giamatti reports, writing "on Yale Club stationery,

wondered why the hell we always had to get so far out in front,"
and we are reminded that the new president had inherited a
restive alumni body, many still resentful of President Brewster's public assertion years earlier, at the time of the May Day
crisis in the spring of 1970 over the Black Panther trials in New
Haven, that he was "skeptical of the ability of black revolutionaries to achieve a fair trial anywhere in the United States."

The reaction of the *Yale Daily News,* as reported by Giamatti, suggests that the adversarial relationship between students and administration that characterized the sixties, reflecting what Brewster called the "monumental scorn" of students
for things as they are, was still present, though perhaps in less
virulent form:

> Giamatti's administration is off to a miserable start. Rather
> than giving us control of our lives, or at least addressing con-
> cerns of students such as the crying need for a student center
> so we can make friends or any of the myriad of other injustices
> that riddle the fabric of the quality of life here, the new ad-
> ministration is insensitive and the future bodes aweful.

"Though one of the best-written of the *News* editorials," Giamatti wryly notes of this mischievous parody, "it was, be fair,
also the first."

Another legacy of the Brewster years, the rise of academic
postmodernism in all of its myriad forms, was particularly
uncongenial to Giamatti, who reports still another reaction:
"Four young members of the faculty in Comparative Literature
wrote an open letter to the *New York Review of Books* proving
that Milton was not talking about evil in *Paradise Lost* but
about irony and the patriarchal abuse of power." These academic tendencies had become sufficiently widespread at Yale,
as on other campuses, that Giamatti as president was largely
obliged to tolerate them, but his distaste for them may have

been part of the reason for one of the first actions of his administration, the dismissal of the ferociously iconoclastic postmodernist dean of the Yale School of Drama, Robert Brustein.

Brustein, a well-known theater critic, had joined the Yale faculty in 1966, the same year as Giamatti. He had been recruited by Kingman Brewster from Columbia, where he had been teaching dramatic literature, to reinvigorate a school that many felt had become hidebound and uncreative. In the intervening years, he had transformed the Yale School of Drama, theretofore a graduate school with a strong academic bias, into a conservatory concerned with developing artists for the American stage; and he had established the Yale Repertory Theatre, a professional company performing experimental new plays as well as classics in avant-garde productions, from which an untenured faculty for the school was largely drawn and where students from the school could test their wings in small parts.

Brustein's productions at the Yale Rep were unfailingly controversial, as he intended them to be. He much preferred, he said, an angry spectator to a sleepy one. While still at Columbia, he had championed a new play called *MacBird*, whose premise (acknowledged as "irresponsible" even by Brustein) was that President Johnson had arranged for President Kennedy's assassination. The instinct to provoke, even shock, carried over into his productions of new plays at Yale. Nor were the classics spared the Brustein treatment. His production of Shakespeare's comedy *As You Like It* concluded with Hymen, the god of marriage customarily represented as a beautiful youth carrying a bridal torch and wearing a veil, singing his song in praise of wedlock, his head adorned with phalluses and his body with four female breasts.

When in 1976 Brustein's second five-year term as dean of the school and director of the Rep came to an end, Brewster had offered him another five-year term. He accepted a two-year extension, subsequently extended to three, with, Brustein believed, an option on his part to extend further for the balance of the five-year period through 1981. When Giamatti took office in 1978, Brustein was entering the third of the five years. During the years of his deanship, personal contact between him and Giamatti had been intermittent, limited largely to meetings of the board of the undergraduate Yale Dramat, on which both served. It is possible—though surely not likely— that they might have become friends, this conservative English professor, a gradualist steeped in traditional values, and this liberal dean, believing (in his own words) that "gradualism [is] a form of compromise" and (borrowing from William Blake) that "the tigers of wrath [are] wiser than the horses of instruction." But they did not. Indeed, by the time Giamatti assumed the presidency of Yale, each had developed a genuine dislike for the other.

Brustein believed that Giamatti lacked character, a conclusion based largely, it seems, on an episode at the faculty meeting in 1969 following the Wright Hall episode. Giamatti had cast what Brustein, a hawk when it came to disciplining unruly students, considered a cynical and spineless vote in favor of leniency for the group of students who had occupied Wright Hall, after he had regaled Brustein throughout the meeting with caustic comments, behind his hand, on the cowardice of his colleagues. Giamatti's conduct was, to be sure, the actor's instinct thoughtlessly misapplied. But so strong an impression did the incident make on Brustein that it caused him to state, when interviewed years later by the search committee, that he did not believe Giamatti had the character to be president of Yale.

There is no record of what Giamatti thought of Brustein's character. Philosophical differences aside (and they were, of course, very great), he simply didn't like him. It was an unfortunate characteristic of Brustein's style to express differences of opinion by disparaging the motives of those who disagreed with him. He did not conceal his disdain for the "purists in the English department" who did not share his postmodernist vision of classical plays. Humanists, he said, "have a vested interest in 'masterpieces'—they are the precious metals of a huge research industry." Giamatti was not alone at Yale in being offended by this abrasive style. In the memoir of his Yale years, Brustein reports a student comment about him in a *New York Times* article: "You know the Sara Lee slogan in the TV commercials, 'Everybody doesn't like something, but nobody doesn't like Sara Lee'? Well, around here that might be paraphrased to read, 'Everybody doesn't like somebody, but nobody doesn't dislike Robert Brustein.'"

Beyond the philosophical gulf that separated Giamatti and Brustein, and the personal animosity between them, there existed a fundamental difference in outlook as to the proper role of the Yale School of Drama within the university. In transforming it from an academic graduate school into a professional conservatory, Brustein had made basic changes. He had persuaded Brewster to eliminate tenure for faculty so that the teaching could be done largely by resident actors in the Repertory Theatre. He had discontinued many of the academic courses previously offered. And he had severely restricted access to the school by undergraduates, who before his tenure had been allowed to join the acting classes with the drama students. This last policy was particularly unwelcome to Giamatti, who had been active as an undergraduate in Yale theater —had, in fact, met his wife while she was a student in the School of Drama.

Giamatti told Brustein in May 1978 that the following academic year would be his last as dean. By Brustein's account, Giamatti specifically stated at that meeting that he wished to see the changes to the School of Drama reversed. But the reason he gave for Brustein's dismissal was that he intended to enforce throughout the university a policy established by Brewster imposing a ten-year limit on Yale deans. Brustein had already served twelve years under a special Brewster dispensation; the dispensation was not to be renewed.

While Brustein believed that he had a legal right to serve until 1981 (doubtful—in the correspondence between Brewster and Brustein in 1976 establishing the two-year extension, Brewster had written vaguely of "the possibility of renewal at the end of that time"), he never sought to assert that right, recognizing that continuation was impossible where important policy differences existed. But he did not go quietly. The change in Brustein's status had not been announced by the university— indeed Giamatti had not yet assumed office—when Brustein in the late spring of 1978 wrote to his faculty informing them that he would be leaving the following spring and referring to the policy changes Giamatti contemplated. His statement reached the press, and before the episode was over, Brustein was quoted as calling Giamatti's policies a "plan to deprofessionalize the drama program."

Giamatti refused to be drawn into a debate. The termination of Brustein's deanship, he said, was based solely on the ten-year limitation for Yale deans; it was "an appointment matter, not a policy matter." Any new policy would come only as a result of study over the coming year. He refused to acknowledge that he had discussed policy changes with Brustein— though there seems no reason to doubt Brustein's assertion that he had. Brustein saw in Giamatti's denial still another example of his flawed character. He had had, he wrote to Giamatti, "the privilege of serving under two Presidents [Brewster and Hanna Gray] of unimpeachable character, honor, and integrity. At present, I do not believe I am associated any longer with an ethical institution."

At the end of the 1978–79 academic year Brustein left Yale, moving to Harvard to head its undergraduate drama program and to reestablish his theater as the American Repertory Theatre at the Loeb Drama Center in Cambridge, where it continues to flourish. At the Yale graduation ceremonies in the spring of 1979, he made what he called his "final scene" in New Haven: he refused to tip his cap to Giamatti when presenting the Drama School graduates, and he refused to address him as "Mr. President."

Giamatti began to assemble his academic team even before assuming the presidency. In March 1978 he named Abraham S. Goldstein as provost to succeed Hanna Gray, who had been appointed president of the University of Chicago effective at the beginning of the 1978–79 academic year. Goldstein's rise from humble beginnings to prominence was not unlike that of Valentine Giamatti. The son of immigrant parents in New York, he had achieved academic success at the City College of New York and at Yale Law School. After a clerkship with the chief justice of the federal appeals court in Washington, D.C., and a period of private practice in that city, he had returned to Yale Law School as a member of the faculty in 1956, becoming a full professor in 1961. He had served as dean from 1970 to 1975, building a reputation as a defender of law and order in the tumultuous campus environment of the early 1970s. In 1978, at the beginning of Giamatti's presidency, he was a Sterling Professor of Law, the most prestigious category of professorship that Yale offers.

He and Giamatti were barely acquainted before he became provost. They were separated in age by a dozen or so years and by academic interests. Giamatti, barely forty, had been an English professor. Goldstein belonged to an older circle of distinguished Yale faculty in the social sciences that included law professor Alexander Bickel, economists James Tobin and Henry Broude, and historian John Morton Blum. It was Broude, adviser to Kingman Brewster and thereafter to Giamatti, who inquired of Goldstein whether he would be interested in being included among those under consideration for appointment as provost. The rationale for his appointment is unclear, but his reputation as a law-and-order executive and as a strong and experienced administrator must have been important factors.

The provost of a university is the academic equivalent of the executive vice president of a business, with jurisdiction running to every aspect of its activities to the extent that the president himself does not exercise it. But it is commonly understood that the provost's principal responsibility is oversight of the budget process. Because budget reform was an urgent priority for the Giamatti administration, Goldstein's role was particularly important, and, working with Giamatti himself and the new vice president for finance and administration, Jerald L. Stevens, he was central to this effort. The three worked as an effective team with positive results in what appeared to be an atmosphere of harmony and mutual confidence until, in the spring of 1979, less than a year into Giamatti's presidency, an event occurred that put an end to Goldstein's tenure as provost and cast doubt upon the working relationship between him and the president.

On April 23, 1979, the *Yale Daily News,* acting on information believed to have been furnished to it by union workmen seeking to embarrass the university, ran a front-page story disclosing that $67,000 in university funds had been spent on what it called "redecoration" of the provost's house in New Haven. At a time when fiscal austerity was the watchword at Yale, this disclosure was embarrassment enough, but the story also asserted that several newly installed fixtures had been relocated because "Mrs. Goldstein did not like the way they looked," and several rooms had been repainted or rewallpapered because she "didn't like the shade."

Goldstein was furious, because he believed the expenditures were well within the program for renovation of the provost's house that had been approved when he accepted his appointment, and because he resented the implied criticism of his wife. His sensitivity was heightened by his belief at the time that he was on the short list for appointment by President Carter to a judgeship on the federal appellate bench, and that the episode might prejudice his chances. He appealed to Giamatti to defend him publicly, and when Giamatti refused, he resigned, stating that "recent conversations with the President have led me to conclude that I do not wish to continue serving in his administration."

It was widely believed at Yale that Giamatti had taken cover because a program of renovation of the president's house was in progress at a cost (though privately funded) of some three times that of the provost's, and Giamatti was at pains to avoid personal embarrassment. Giamatti, in accepting the resignation, suggested that the reasons were otherwise. "Differences of perspective, in my opinion," he said, "have been growing over a period of months." Some understood this to mean that Giamatti believed Goldstein was operating too independently of the president. A less charitable view was that Giamatti, younger and less experienced than his provost, resented what he took to be Goldstein's air of superiority over his boss, however unintended; and that a question was raised whether Giamatti was capable of working with strong subordinates. Giamatti was also said to be annoyed that Goldstein would even consider accepting a judicial appointment so soon after becoming provost.

Whatever the truth, the episode did not reflect well on

Giamatti. The expenditures in question, most of which were for structural or permanent improvements, were, after all, being made to Yale property, of which the Goldsteins were only temporary occupants. And assuming that the newspaper account of Mrs. Goldstein's role was true, she was a novelist, not an interior decorator, and she cannot have been the first to have had second thoughts when paint or wallpaper did not look the same on the wall as it had on the swatch from which the choice was made. A seasoned and confident leader would have stood up for his provost and defended the renovation program, to both houses, as in the best interests of the university. And if he wanted to replace Goldstein for other reasons, he would not have allowed the change to occur at that time and under those circumstances.

Goldstein's sudden departure left a dangerous vacancy on the team Giamatti had assembled to deal with the budget crisis, and it was important that it be filled promptly. Giamatti turned to Sterling Professor of French Georges May, dean of Yale College from 1963 to 1971, a seasoned administrator with broad knowledge of the workings of Yale. May agreed to assume the post for two years. Over the brief period that he served as provost, and thus *ex officio* as chairman of the crucially important budget committee, Yale achieved a balanced budget for the first time in a decade. May did not accomplish this alone, of course, but his contribution was essential. When his two-year term ended in 1981, he was succeeded as provost by William C. Brainard, a professor of economics, who had served as the faculty representative on the budget committee. Brainard remained provost for the rest of Giamatti's presidency.

The other key figure in the assault on the budget deficit was Jerald L. Stevens, whom Giamatti appointed at the beginning of his term to the newly created office of vice president for finance and administration. Stevens, a 1963 graduate of Yale

College, came to the Giamatti team from Massachusetts state government, where he had served as commissioner of the Department of Welfare and thereafter as secretary of human services in the administration of Governor Michael S. Dukakis. A skilled financial manager with a degree from the Harvard Business School, he remained at Yale until the end of 1982, when the corner had been turned on budget reform.

In 1979 Giamatti succeeded in coaxing back to Yale his old friend and Yale classmate John Wilkinson, who in 1974 had resigned as dean of undergraduate affairs to become headmaster of Hopkins Grammar Day Prospect Hill School in New Haven. Wilkinson returned as the university officer for development and alumni affairs, and when in 1981 Henry Chauncey, Jr., who had been secretary of the university during the Brewster years, resigned that post, Wilkinson was appointed to succeed him. He remained secretary throughout the Giamatti presidency. He was succeeded in the development and alumni affairs job, now a vice presidency, by Terry M. Holcombe, returning from Columbia to Yale, where he had been the last executive director of the Campaign for Yale, the university's capital fund drive in the 1970s.

In 1979 Giamatti appointed Howard Lamar, a professor of history, to succeed Brewster appointee Horace Taft as dean of Yale College. Lamar served until 1985, when he was succeeded by biology professor Sidney Altman.

Henry Broude, the Yale economist who had served as special assistant to President Brewster, was kept on in that capacity, occupying the only other office in the presidential suite in Woodbridge Hall. Broude was, and is, discreet to the point of secretiveness about the nature of his service to Giamatti, but physical proximity alone would suggest that he played an important role behind the scenes in the Giamatti administration.

The Homilies

During his presidency of Yale, Giamatti articulated a compelling vision of the nature and purpose of a university and of a liberal education. To this task he brought an unsurpassed eloquence that allowed him to reach and influence even those who never saw or heard him. One Yale alumnus was so struck by the high sentiment and freshness of expression of Giamatti's talk to the incoming freshmen in the spring of 1980, as reprinted in the *Yale Alumni Magazine,* that he clipped its closing passage and put it in the flap of his pocket diary, where it remained for reference from year to year as old diaries were discarded and replaced by new ones. Here is the passage:

> A liberal education is a process of self-knowledge for the purpose of shared civility. It should foster a skepticism of the Apocalyptic or Coercive Style, a tolerance for other beliefs and peoples, a passion for excellence and equity, a respect for the dignity of the individual. . . . A liberal education is a process, whereby we each make ourselves part of a commonality that respects the majesty and integrity of the individual talent. To engage the process you have only to embrace the

proposition that by testing yourself against the new you will be made, by yourself, renewed.

I welcome you to the manifold pleasures of the spirit of renaissance.

Giamatti's vision was set forth in a series of talks to undergraduates—two each year, one to incoming freshmen in the fall, the other to graduating seniors in the spring. Maynard Mack called them homilies—informal discourses on a moral theme. But their apparent informality masks the exquisite care with which they were prepared. The first drafts were usually the work of the summer on Martha's Vineyard. These drafts were circulated for comment among a small group of friends and colleagues, then reworked until they embodied Giamatti's best product. They were, as he meant them to be, the highest expression of the values of his presidency.

Giamatti's eloquence was even more dazzling when experienced in his charismatic presence. Those who attended his talk to graduating seniors in the spring of 1981 were treated to an example. He was speaking of coercion, and his audience was cautioned to beware the influence of Ralph Waldo Emerson and his worship of "self-reliance and original action" deriving from transcendental harmony with the highest laws of Nature. "To Emerson," Giamatti said,

> we owe the spirit of Puritan America that has survived to today, the smug, abstract moralism that is distrustful of any accommodation, that is always certain of its righteousness. . . . In another creed, his self-reliance would be the sin of pride.
>
> Emerson's views are those of a brazen adolescent. We ought to be rid of them.

Ralph Waldo Emerson, the silver-haired sage of Concord, a "brazen adolescent"? The verve, almost gleeful, with which Giamatti delivered that sentence dramatized beyond anything the written page can convey the splendid audacity of the statement.

In the introduction to the last and most complete collection of his speeches while president of Yale, *A Free and Ordered Space: The Real World of the University*, Giamatti asserts that universities have a responsibility to redefine and reassert publicly their nature and purpose. When they are not challenged to justify themselves, he says, "they stiffen up and lose their evolving complementarity to other American institutions." Giamatti believed that for the thirty or so years following World War II universities had failed in this responsibility, creating a vacuum into which "have rushed all manner of fatuous or reactionary critical accounts of higher education's mission, explanations whose surface plausibility and essential wrongheadedness have found a willing and eager national audience." Giamatti does not give examples of these wrongheaded accounts of the mission of the university, but we can find them elsewhere in his writings: that the university exists for the purpose of remedying the social ills of the community; that it is the duty of undergraduate education to offer "pre-professional" training for a career; that the university should inculcate "morality" in its students.

Universities, Giamatti says, are not perceived as leading because they are not themselves being led; at best they are being competently managed. Management—the capacity to handle ad hoc problems, to neutralize various constituencies, to balance the budget—is an essentially protective act. Leadership, on the other hand, is an essentially moral act: to assert a vision of the institution and to persuade the larger community of the wisdom and validity of the vision. He himself, he writes, does "not pretend to fill the vacuum that I . . . assert exists with regard to higher education's nature and purpose." This disclaimer is disingenuous; of course he does. In the speeches to students—Giamatti customarily spoke less philosophically to convocations of alumni and other audiences—he seeks to articulate his view of what the university should be and what it, and the education it offers, are for.

Giamatti's speeches on the nature and purpose of the university and a liberal education, like his academic writings, reflect his etymological bent. Their texture is created by careful use of a vocabulary in which words with a common root take on mutually enriching meanings in various contexts, and key words with different roots have meanings that relate to and illuminate each other. Paraphrase obscures; it dims Giamatti's eloquence and it dilutes his meaning. As always, it is better to let Giamatti speak for himself. Thus, on the nature of the university:

> Its essence is as a place of . . . civil conversation, . . . where values of all kinds are meant to collide, to contest, to be debated, disagreed about—freely, openly, civilly (as opposed to coercively). . . . When that conversation . . . is told that it must cease because there is only one Truth and it is Complete, then the institution in its essence is chilled and its life threatened.
>
> Institutions of higher education must be . . . shapely, free and ordered . . . or they will not be able to teach the interplay of freedom and order that shapes an individual or a society. . . . A civilized order is the precondition of freedom, and freedom —of belief, speech, and choice—the goal of responsible order.

The key words are those that derive from *civility* (*civil, civilly, civilized*); *coercion* (*coercively*); *freedom*; and *order*. As we shall see, these words and the concepts they embody figure centrally not only in Giamatti's view of the nature of the university but also in his conviction as to the nature and purpose of a liberal education. It will thus be instructive to pause and consider their significances before proceeding.

Giamatti himself provides a gloss on the word *civility*. "It has to do," he says, "with decency and mutual respect and, finally, with a free and ordered common life—or civilization." He might have added that its Latin root—*civilis*—means "pertaining to a citizen," for *civility* carries that sense when Giamatti speaks of the purpose of a liberal education. These meanings of *civility* are, of course, related, and all of them are intended to resonate whenever Giamatti uses the word.

If *civility* has to do with "mutual respect," *coercion* is its opposite. It is the word Giamatti uses when he means the assertive style of those "who lust for the simple answers of doctrine or decree." They are, he says "on the Left and the Right. They are the terrorists of the mind." They include the religious Moral Majority, so vocal in the 1980s, from whose "maw," Giamatti told the incoming freshman class in 1981,

> come those who presume to know what justice for all is; come those who presume to know which books are fit to read, which television programs are fit to watch, which textbooks will serve for all the young; come spilling those who presume to know what God alone knows, which is when human life begins. . . . There is no debate, no discussion, no dissent. They know. There is only one set of overreaching political and spiritual and social beliefs; whatever view does not conform to these views is by definition relativistic, negative, secular, immoral, against the family, anti–free enterprise, Un-American. What nonsense.
>
> What dangerous, malicious nonsense.

But there is also a Moral Minority. They are

> the voices that for every cause—social, political, academic, sexual, religious, or ethnic—demand satisfaction NOW. These voices are scornful of complexity, indifferent to ambiguity, contemptuous of competitive views or values. . . . Hungering for Decree, for Absolutes, these voices are encouraged because they are said to be "idealistic." What they are is precisely not idealistic, but, in their simplifying, reductionistic.

Coercion is not less so when practiced by "idealists." Nor, as Giamatti's assessment of Ralph Waldo Emerson tells us, by icons. Those who reject coercion, Giamatti told the graduating class of 1982, are those who (quoting from his late colleague, law professor Alexander Bickel)

> fix their "eyes on that middle distance, where values are provisionally held, are tested, and evolve—derived from the morality of process, which is the morality of consent." . . .
> Fear like Hell the self-inflicted blindness of self-righteousness, where all perspective is foreshortened and all doubt is denied, and keep your eyes on the middle distance, where means and process live.

Less needs to be said about *freedom* and *order*. When Giamatti speaks of freedom in the context of the university, he means "freedom of belief, speech and choice." When he speaks of order, he is referring to what he calls "civility's curbing rein," the "spirit . . . tolerant, respectful and candid" that is "essential to sustain the freedom of the mind inquiring." Freedom and order must coexist: "A civilized order is the precondition of freedom, and freedom . . . the goal of responsible order."

> There is no true freedom without order; we learn that there are limits to our freedom. . . . If there were, on the one hand, no restraints at all, only anarchy of intellect and chaos of community would result. On the other hand, if all were restraint, and release of inquiry and thought were stifled, only a death of the spirit and denial of any freedom could result. There must be an interplay of restraint and release, of order and freedom.

As we have seen, Giamatti defines civility as having to do "with a free and ordered common life—or civilization." The university in which freedom and order properly coexist is a "civilization."

With all of this as background, it is time to turn to Giamatti's concept of the product that it is the purpose of the university to offer—a liberal education—what it is and what it is for. He tells us first what it is not. It is not political: "A liberal education has nothing to do with those political labels *liberal* and *conservative* that some so lovingly stitch on to every idea they pull off, or put on, the rack." It stands, in the words of the nineteenth-century English educational theorist John Henry Newman, "on its own pretensions, . . . independent of sequel." "If you pursue the study of anything," Giamatti says, "because you press toward a professional goal, then you are pursuing not a liberal education, but rather something else." This is the principle on which he based his proposals, so unpopular with some alumni, for severe restrictions on varsity athletics. A university should, he believed, "no more encourage a professionalism of spirit in athletics in our undergraduates than we encourage a professional view of the purpose of an undergraduate education."

What, then, is a liberal education? It is, Giamatti says, the "educational process by which the mind is ordered so that it may be open." A liberal education seeks to replicate within the individual the balance that should exist within the university itself. "There must be an interplay of restraint and release, of order and freedom, in our individual lives and in our life together." "Your education here," he says to the incoming freshmen in 1981, "intends to bring you to comprehend the responsibilities and the pleasures of that essential, grand connection."

And what is its purpose? "A liberal education," he says, "is a process of self-knowledge for the purpose of shared civility." We have seen that *civility* is the word Giamatti uses to describe the condition under which freedom and order are in proper balance, and that meaning is certainly present. But the Latin root of the word *civility*—*civilis*—carries the sense of pertaining to a citizen. That sense is predominant here, for as Giamatti clearly and repeatedly states in his speeches, the ultimate goal of a liberal education is constructive citizenship:

> There is nothing more enduring and more necessary for a full and decent life . . . than an education that sets as the end of intellectual development a civic goal, that places as the purpose of making a good mind, the making of a good citizen. . . . How . . . we choose a civic role for ourselves . . . is the basic purpose of an education in a democracy.

In so defining the purpose of a liberal education, Giamatti reaches back to the English Renaissance of the sixteenth century that was the center of his own scholarly interests. We are referred to the educational writings of the man Giamatti calls the greatest of Elizabethan schoolmasters, Richard Mulcaster, headmaster of Merchant Taylors' School in London, where Edmund Spenser received his preuniversity education. Central to what Giamatti calls Mulcaster's "humanism" is the belief that true education shapes the private man for the public good. This is the ideal brought to America by the first settlers in the New World, the ideal that comes down to us through Jefferson and the other Founding Fathers.

A like lineage for the purpose of a liberal education is traced in the papers of A. Whitney Griswold, Yale's president in the 1950s, one of the few outspoken public voices for liberal education in those years. But when he expresses its purpose, he means something different. "The purpose of a liberal education," he writes, "is to expand to the limit the individual's capacity—and desire—for self-improvement, for seeking and finding enjoyment and meaning in everything he does. Thus does liberal education serve the purpose of democracy."

It is not immediately clear how the second sentence follows from the first. Elsewhere Griswold adds that a liberal education aims to develop moral and intellectual powers to be exercised not only to achieve greater personal happiness, but also the "greater benefit of [one's] fellow men." All political philosophies, he writes,

> try to draw the line between the opportunities and respon-
> sibilities of the individual and those of society, but none draws
> it so subtly in accordance with reality as democracy. And what
> is that reality? It is that for nine thousand years society has
> depended upon its members as individuals for those creative
> achievements of mind and spirit that have guided it along the
> path of civilization. The spark from heaven falls. Who picks it
> up? The crowd? Never. The individual? Always. It is he and he
> alone, as artist, inventor, explorer, scholar, scientist, spiritual
> leader, or statesman, who stands nearest to the source of life
> and transmits its essence to his fellow men.

It is in this way that the person with a liberal education can contribute to the "greater benefit of his fellow men" and that a liberal education serves the purpose of democracy.

There is a slight whiff of elitism here, more readily detect-able in our time than it was in Griswold's. Much more relevant to our own contentious age is Giamatti's formulation that the purpose of a liberal education is to teach men and women the art of tolerant discourse so that they can engage constructively in the good work of the world.

What is the use of such a formulation? Is it true, or is it simply another pipe dream of one of those college professors who, as a stalwart of Tammany Hall once said, "go up in a balloon to think"? It is certainly a vision. As was amply demon-strated during the most painful episode of Giamatti's presi-dency, the protracted and bitter strike of Yale's white-collar employees in the fall of 1984, when Giamatti himself was the target of vituperative abuse by members of the Yale commu-nity, the university of "civil conversation" and the society of persons within it trained to "shared civility" are a university

and society that never was. But Giamatti would have acknowledged (though in practice he found it hard to bear) that high
purpose in the world of fallen Man is always a vision; no one
knew it better than his own poet Spenser: "Nothing is sure,
that growes on earthly ground." The vision he puts forward of
the proper nature of a modern university and the nature and
purpose of the education it exists to offer is a proud and coherent, if aspirational, one. Its articulation is a unique legacy
of Giamatti's presidency.

But was Giamatti's vision any more than an academician's
idyll, useless as a guide for leadership of a complex modern
"multiversity" of competing constituencies? Its president must
be, as Clark Kerr argues in his classic definition of that term,
a "mediator-initiator"—an advocate for progress, but also a
keeper of the peace. Many of Giamatti's thoughtful colleagues
believed it was far too simple to substitute the "moral" act of
vision for the "protective" act of management. When late in
Giamatti's presidency dissension and unrest reminiscent of the
sixties returned to the Yale campus, they missed the steady
hand of a seasoned and confident manager.

Budget Reform

During most of the presidency of Kingman Brewster, Yale ran operating deficits. They were generally small —less than a million dollars annually in budgets in the hundreds of millions—and they were justified as necessary to remedy what the administration regarded as "educational deficits," lingering from earlier years, in the recruitment and promotion of distinguished faculty and the expansion and improvement of programs. In the early 1970s, however, the deficits began to grow larger—$1.8 million in 1969–70, $2.6 million in 1970–71, $1.2 million in 1971–72. Richard N. Cooper, who became provost in 1972 for a two-year stint, was told by the Yale Corporation to balance the budget during his term in office, and he did, exercising an ability, as he said, to "say no in nineteen ways" to requests for new hires, promotions, and upgraded programs. Some 550 staff and faculty positions were eliminated. This was the period to which Giamatti referred when he said that "in the faculty . . . it seemed as if it were raining every day."

By the 1975–76 fiscal year, however, annual deficits of more than a million dollars had returned, reaching in 1976–77 the alarming figure of $6.6 million, reflecting, among other things, the high inflation and escalating energy costs of the time. Moreover, the deficits were incurred notwithstanding the fact that Yale was overspending from its endowment for current purposes. In the 1960s Yale, like many other institutions, began to measure the performance of its endowment on a so-called "total return" basis—that is, by adding appreciation in market value to income earned in the form of interest and dividends. The percentage of the endowment available for current expenditures was to be determined by a formula called the University Equation, a weighted average of the percentages of the endowment constituting total returns in recent years. When the formula was established, it was thought that it would result in the expenditure annually of not more than 5 percent of the endowment. But in a falling stock market, when the annual total return is reduced or even negative, including earlier years in the formula has the effect of producing a percentage higher than the most recent total returns. Over the ten-year period ending in 1976–77, Yale spent an average of nearly 6 percent of its endowment annually for current purposes, more than the endowment was earning even on a total return basis.

Yale in these years was also neglecting prudent maintenance of its physical assets, particularly serious on a campus of predominantly neo-Gothic buildings, with a lot of expensive-to-maintain stonework and leaded glass. Accounting principles applicable to a university do not require inclusion of an allowance for depreciation as an expense in the operating budget; only amounts actually spent are included. It is thus possible to achieve a balanced budget (or, in Yale's case, to come nearer to doing so) without adequate provision for building maintenance. In tight financial times this is a great temptation, and Yale succumbed to it.

During the academic year 1977–78, at the direction of the Yale Corporation, Hanna Gray's administration conducted a thorough assessment of Yale's financial situation that resulted in a lengthy report issued by the Corporation in late 1977 entitled *Achieving Financial Equilibrium at Yale*. It set forth a concept of "financial equilibrium" that was to govern Yale's budgets during the Giamatti administration and beyond.

> The concept is that current operations and capital expenditures must draw down only such an amount from endowment and physical assets as will preserve in perpetuity the purchasing power of endowment and the useful life of physical assets. . . . The preservation of the real purchasing power of the endowment requires that spending from endowment for current and capital purposes must be at a level that is no more than the long-term, real [that is, after adjustment of the endowment to compensate for inflation] rate of return from the investment of the endowment. Higher spending than the real rate of return means that current generations of beneficiaries are being favored over future generations. Likewise, the under-maintenance of physical assets favors the present over the future.

Certain budgeting ground rules were established in the 1977 report with considerable specificity. On the income side, spending from endowment was to be limited by a formula that, based on various assumptions, would reduce the percentage of endowment available for current purposes from 5.6 percent in 1977–78 to 4.5 percent in 1982–83 and keep it there. If the assumptions proved too optimistic, a more stringent limitation might have to be imposed. If the performance of the endowment exceeded expectations, the 4.5 percent limitation would nonetheless remain in effect. On the expense side, a greater contingency fund would have to be budgeted, capital and operating reserves depleted during the Brewster years would have to be restored, and a fund would have to be established to provide for maintenance and replacement of physical assets that could no longer be deferred. All this would have to be accomplished without any reduction in current programs and activities. Without severe corrective action by the new administration, these new ground rules were projected to result in operating deficits over the five-year period from 1978 to 1983 totaling nearly $85 million. These would be deficits, the report concluded, that Yale could not finance.

Yale must instead initiate basic changes in policies, modes of operation, and educational programs beyond any that had yet been attempted, even in the recent years of retrenchment, with the goal of achieving financial equilibrium as soon as possible. Specifically, the new administration was instructed to achieve a fully balanced budget not later than 1980–81 and to limit total deficits in the intervening two years to not more than $7 million. Giamatti had been serving as a member of a special faculty administration committee that had been meeting for months to consider options and alternatives to meet these goals and that would continue to serve in the new administration. He knew what had to be done. We saw him in an earlier chapter holding court on the subject in the nave of the Sterling Library: "Seven million dollars in reductions. . . . SEVEN MILLION DOLLARS. It's incredible." But his administration accomplished it. How?

The task was put in the hands of a small budget committee chaired by the provost, which met biweekly for several hours. Giamatti was not a member, but he attended most of the meetings, staying constantly involved and in touch. Steps to tighten cash management could be implemented immediately. In a reversal of prior laxness, students were not allowed to register for classes until their tuition had been paid—not a huge saving in dollars, but a signal to the Yale community of financial resolve. Overhead rates on government research grants were renegotiated, resulting in significant additional revenues. A modest increase in the number of students in Yale College and improved results in alumni giving were also pieces in the program to achieve financial equilibrium. But these steps could be no more than a beginning. The fundamental fact was that the ongoing level of educational and administrative expenses to which Yale had committed itself could not be supported by its revenues. Yale had to be downsized, its staffing brought into line with its resources.

Rational downsizing demands a careful analysis of the needs of every part of the university, a process requiring time. So in the first year of the Giamatti presidency savings were achieved largely by an across-the-board freeze on new hires and the filling of vacancies, exceptions made only to meet manifest needs—enough doctors in the University Health Service, for example—after stringent review. Such a freeze is not, of course, a discriminating weapon: positions are left open that rational analysis would dictate should be filled, and expendable positions remain filled simply because attrition has not vacated them. But in the second and third budget years a rational pattern of staffing was developed that Yale could afford until growing resources permitted necessary salary adjustments and the restoring of eliminated positions.

Giamatti's personal role in all this was indispensable. He was—and was seen by all to be—fully involved in and supportive of the process. There were no end runs around the provost for special treatment: Giamatti had a nice way of saying no. Where necessary, feathers were smoothed and painful cuts justified. Members of the Yale community knew that Giamatti understood the university's teaching mission and was deeply committed to it. They knew that he would not let the budget cutters do anything fundamentally unsound.

Giamatti's hands-on attention to reform of the budget process was accompanied by diligent efforts to repair relations with alumni, frayed in the Brewster administration. He was on the road constantly, as often as once a month, visiting cities all over the country, meeting informally with alumni leaders, speaking to the local Yale Club, challenging and charming the members afterward in give-and-take sessions.

Throughout all this, Giamatti never lost his incomparable sense of humor. Speaking in 1985 to a group of Yale Law School alumni shortly after the retirement of Harry Wellington as dean, long after the financial travail of the early years of his administration had passed, he recalled a dream he had had five years earlier, after a day in which he had met at lunch with all the deans and officers of Yale. At the lunch, he said,

> We had spoken of the limited resources of the University and as the conversation progressed, the Deans had gradually fallen silent. I was sure the reason was that each wished to ponder how best they might each sacrifice out of their respective schools for the general or common good. I was moved by their silence and thoughtful care and I spoke, I thought rather feelingly and rather well, of how we would all be one team, working together to allocate wisely and fairly the real but limited resources, so that the larger community, the University as a whole, would be able to pursue excellence in a fashion as unimpeded as possible. I said that as a team, we would play, all of us, Deans and Officers, a role as a model for the University community for co-operation and collegiality in a time of stress and uncertainty. It was, if I may say so, a strong speech, from the heart, though I recognize that you had to be there.

The dream that Giamatti said he had had the following night was of a phantasmagorical baseball game between the deans and the administration of the university, in which the deans were always at bat and the administration (called the Feeders, the original name for pitchers) always in the field. The president was the pitcher and the provost was the catcher. By the end of the game all of the deans had congregated around second base, which "was of normal size and was marked in huge letters—THE SHRINKING PIE, OR WHAT REMAINS WHEN THE FEEDERS FINISH FEEDING." Giamatti's account continues:

> Many of the Deans were tagging the bag, digging their spikes into an edge, or in search of an edge; others were sliding in spikes up, trying for a corner. Two Deans were intensely talking to the large, shadowy figure who stood nearby, the Umpire, who wore a tiny, round, short-billed cap with YALE CORPORA- TION written on it. . . . The Deans arguing with the Umpire were making a case that they should have a second base apiece. The shortstop, a position held down by the Vice President for De- velopment, was surrounded by three Deans who were offering him all sorts of inducements to jump teams and to come play for them.

By the 1980–81 fiscal year the Yale budget was in balance as scheduled. The deficits for the two preceding years had been $2.5 million and $1.9 million, respectively, a total of $4.4 mil- lion, comfortably below the $7 million limit that the 1977 re- port had imposed. But in order to achieve these results, it had been necessary largely to defer the expenditures on the physi- cal plant that the concept of financial equilibrium required. In 1981 this problem began to be addressed, when Yale borrowed $10 million on a long-term basis to renovate and modernize some of the most neglected of its buildings over the following two years. Debt service—interest and amortization of principal —would be included in the operating budget as incurred over the term of the loan, but this method of financing maintenance made it possible to spread its cost over several budget cycles. Giamatti now had something new to laugh about. He would be remembered, he said, as Bart the Refurbisher, the man with all his ducts in a row. "If my name goes on anything, it will be the Giamatti Memorial Wiring System."

Yale's operating budget continued in balance for the rest of

Giamatti's tenure. When he departed in 1986, Yale's endowment was more than twice what it had been when he became president, and annual gifts from alumni had also doubled. Faculty salaries were now competitive. Giamatti was justifiably proud of the accomplishment of his administration. "Yale was viewed as a ship foundering in high seas when I became president," he said just before he left. "Now, I hope, it's viewed as a ship sailing with purpose and majesty."

Full economic recovery at Yale was by no means achieved during the Giamatti administration. Deferred maintenance remained a serious problem—the beginning made with the 1981 bond issue was hardly more than symbolic. New construction had to be deferred, as did reforms in curriculum and program development. The situation worsened during the brief tenure of Giamatti's successor, Benno Schmidt, who had to endure the economic slump of the late 1980s and early 1990s that ushered in the Clinton administration. Richard Levin, who took office in 1993, was the first Yale president in more than two decades to enjoy a strong economy and stock market, which have made it possible for him to address the deficiencies and unmet needs he inherited from his predecessors. There was still much to be done at the end of the Giamatti years. But the house was in order.

For all of Kingman Brewster's remarkable successes as president of Yale, he had left the place in a financial shambles, with attendant low morale. Budget details did not interest him; they were for the provost to worry about. This neglect did not do much harm in the 1960s, when the stock market was generally robust, inflation was low, and universities were the beneficiaries of generous government grants for research. But Brewster's lack of interest in budgetary issues continued into the 1970s, when the external climate began to change for the worse. His longtime provost Charles Taylor remembers a conversation with him one day in the early 1970s on the ferry from Woods Hole to Martha's Vineyard, when he warned Brewster of budget troubles ahead. Brewster didn't want to hear it. Do what you have to do, he said. A systematic analysis of Yale's financial situation was undertaken by Hanna Gray only after Brewster had left, and a program to address it came only with Giamatti. It is said that Kingman Brewster saved Yale in the 1960s, and so he did. But Giamatti had to save it again, in a different time and from a different affliction.

The President and New Haven

Stormy relations between Yale and New Haven go back to the early days of the college. By the middle of the nineteenth century confrontations between students and citizens of New Haven were frequent and often violent, on occasion resulting in fatalities. As late as the 1920s such confrontations still occurred. Henry Chauncey, Jr., secretary of the university during Kingman Brewster's presidency and instrumental in nurturing constructive town-gown relations during the later Brewster years, recalled in 1973 in an article published in the *Yale Alumni Magazine* a story told by a family friend who graduated from Yale around the end of World War I—full of exaggeration and hyperbole, to be sure, even in part apocryphal, but illustrative of the tensions of the time. The friend described

> the occasion on which the Yankee Division marched through New Haven to celebrate the end of the war. It turned out that the Yankee Division had never actually left the United States, and sitting in the windows were many Yale students who had fought in some of the worst battles. The Yale students started to boo and hiss and throw things at the Yankee Division, and

the result was a huge riot in which the city of New Haven drew up a cannon on the Green facing the Yale campus. . . . All the windows on the College Street side of the University were broken by the townspeople, and the Yale President . . . stood in the middle of the Old Campus with a sword and said, "Gentlemen, defend yourselves!"

By Giamatti's time, violence on that scale was a thing of the past, but as we saw in the St. Patrick's Day snowball riot during his undergraduate days, any disturbance that required intervention by the New Haven police could turn bloody.

If the old level of violence in town-gown relations disappeared, however, another characteristic of the relationship did not: an absence of involvement by the university in the concerns of the community. The sixteen years (1954–1969) when Richard C. Lee was mayor of the city may have constituted an exception. Lee was director of the Yale News Bureau when he was elected, and he had many friends within the university, some of whom he appointed to city boards. A notable example was Yale's president, A. Whitney Griswold, who was appointed as vice chairman of the Citizens Action Commission, a body of civic and business leaders created by Lee to serve as a sounding board for his proposals and to legitimize his decisions. Lee and Griswold had been good friends when Lee worked for Yale and Griswold was a Yale history professor, and their friendship led to negotiations that resulted in the purchase by Yale from the city in the late 1950s of Hillhouse High School and two adjacent city schools on Broadway, providing the mayor with cash to finance new high school facilities elsewhere and Yale with a site in the heart of the campus for the construction of two new residential colleges completed in the 1960s, Morse and Ezra Stiles.

But the relationship between the city and the university during the Lee administration existed only at the top, between the mayor and Yale's president, and after 1963, when Griswold died (indeed even earlier, for relations between the two men cooled after charges of police brutality during the 1959 snowball riot), university involvement with the city diminished. At Harvard, where a similarly lukewarm relationship existed with the city of Cambridge, the university's attitude was variously described as a policy of "minimal impact" and "protective detachment." Both phrases might have been applied to Yale's attitude toward New Haven, but institutional indifference may be a more accurate description.

In 1973 the distant relationship between university and city resulted in a crisis. Since women had first been admitted as students in Yale College in 1969, the university had been seeking ways to increase their number without significantly reducing the number of male undergraduates. A basic problem was the need for adequate housing. By the early 1970s Yale had assembled a suitable site and a promise of funding from a generous alumnus for the construction of two new residential colleges immediately adjacent to the existing campus. Approval by the city was needed, under an ordinance later declared illegal, for any project that would create a tax-exempt facility on previously taxable property, and in early 1973 approval was denied by the board of aldermen. Various reasons were given, prime among them Yale's refusal to make payments in lieu of taxes on its tax-exempt educational properties. There is also some reason to believe that the university unwittingly got caught in a cross fire between political factions in the city over control of patronage in the aftermath of the Lee administration, whose extensive program of federally funded urban redevelopment had provided enough patronage for everybody. But surely the city's resentment at what it perceived as Yale's condescending indifference to New Haven and its problems played a major part. "They thought they owned us," said the

Democratic town chairman, Arthur Barbieri. "They are going to have to realize that we are not peasants and they are not the manor on the hill. They are going to have to come down off their high horse and change their relationship with us."

Kingman Brewster asked the secretary of the university, Sam Chauncey, a longtime resident of New Haven, for advice on how to improve relations with the city. Better mutual understanding was needed, Chauncey replied, and better communications at a staff level, where potential conflicts could be anticipated and ameliorated. Chauncey was directed to initiate appropriate steps to achieve these goals, and an Office of Community Relations was established in the secretary's office under the leadership of Chauncey's assistant Peter Halsey, a Yale graduate with family roots in the New Haven area.

By the time Giamatti became president in 1978, the efforts of this new office had begun to bear fruit. Yale was bringing its influence to bear among alumni and others in the business community to help the city accomplish its development goals, though direct financial support for these projects was limited by the straitened financial circumstances of the university, and by Giamatti's fundamental lack of sympathy with the use of university funds for city development. Yale had also led a successful lobbying effort for the passage of legislation, extremely beneficial to New Haven, under which the State of Connecticut reimburses cities and towns in part for property taxes lost to educational uses. What was missing was a means of bridging the cultural gap between a working-class blue-collar city population, of which the dominant group was Italian-American, and what was widely perceived as an elitist university. Giamatti was uniquely suited to provide that bridge.

We have seen that even as an undergraduate Giamatti had access to Italian neighborhoods, off-limits to most Yale students, where his father and grandfather were remembered. He

continued to be a familiar figure in these neighborhoods as a
faculty member. He was, of course, fluent in Italian. He was,
moreover, a regular guy. Unlike many of his faculty colleagues,
he lived in New Haven. He was, everyone knew, a baseball
fanatic. He moved comfortably among the "townies"—the bar-
ber, the small shop proprietor, the cab driver. By the time he
had become president of Yale, some New Haven old-timers
had begun to "remember" him as a boy in the city. He was
associated with the much beloved Italian-American politician
Ella Grasso, who became governor of Connecticut in 1974 after a career in Congress. Grasso, who had never lived in New
Haven, had, it was said, been Giamatti's babysitter when they
both lived in the same tenement building. That myth perhaps
had its origin in the fact that Grasso *had* sat for baby Bart in
South Hadley, where, as Ella Tambussi, the daughter of Italian
immigrants, she had been a student at Mount Holyoke College
and a friend of the Giamatti family. The logic seems to have
been that since Bart "grew up" in New Haven and Grasso was
his babysitter, she must have lived there too. It didn't matter
that it was fiction. It exerted a powerful spell on the minds of
many Italian-American New Haveners.

There was continued contact with members of the Italian-
American community after Giamatti became president of Yale.
His friend Guido Calabresi, the distinguished law professor,
whom Giamatti later appointed dean of the Yale Law School,
remembers an episode at a party at his farm in suburban
Woodbridge. An elderly Italian neighbor asked to be introduced to Yale's new president. Giamatti asked the man in Italian where he was from, and when he was told, he remarked
that his grandfather had come from a town just two villages
away. "No," the man said, "three villages," and he named them.
The startled Yale president had to admit that he stood cor-
rected. "It was marvelous," Calabresi recalls.

But when in 1979 Biagio DiLieto (always called Ben) was elected mayor of New Haven, Giamatti's—and Yale's—identification with the city's Italian-American community was dramatically intensified. DiLieto had been New Haven's police chief earlier in the 1970s, and those at Yale who had worked with him had found him cooperative and constructive. Unlike his two predecessors as mayor, one of whom was a Yale graduate, he regarded the university not as the enemy but as the city's greatest natural resource. He would not, he said, call upon Yale, as earlier mayors had done, to make payments to the city in lieu of taxes. He would instead seek to establish a partnership with the university under which the city would look for support in other ways. The Giamatti administration got off on the right foot with the new mayor by arranging for him to be inaugurated in Woolsey Hall, Yale's magisterial large auditorium. DiLieto and Giamatti became friends and collaborators.

Even before DiLieto became mayor, the new Yale president had taken an interest in the city's schools. While a faculty member he had visited many of them; he had served as a teacher in the Yale Summer High School program. This led to his participation in the creation, shortly before he became president, of the Yale–New Haven Teachers Institute, a joint venture with the city, sponsored by Yale, in which members of the university's faculty and teachers in the city's schools come together in mutually enriching seminars to design curriculum and exchange experience and strengths. Giamatti believed that bringing Yale's educational and human resources to bear on city problems was the most effective contribution the university could make to the community. His enthusiastic support of the Institute throughout his presidency, providing invaluable leadership at the top, was instrumental in its success in attracting foundation and corporate support, and eventually its own endowment. It continues today as a national model for programs of its kind.

Giamatti's interest in the public schools also resulted in the restoration of the Sterling Scholarships for New Haven students to attend Yale, the program from which Giamatti's father had benefited as a boy. The 1979 honors dinner for New Haven high school students was held in Yale's major dining facility, the Commons, on which occasion the president of the Wilbur Cross High School student council declared that "the symbol of Yale–New Haven relations in the 1970s is A. Bartlett Giamatti."

There were other initiatives. In the spring of 1981, an annual event on the Yale campus called Communiversity Day was inaugurated to bring the people of Yale and New Haven together, an occasion that is still celebrated. During the Giamatti-DiLieto years, a highlight of the celebration was a carefully choreographed human chess game, in which the Yale president and the New Haven mayor, adorned in the trappings of royalty, were the two kings. That spring, the semiannual plenary assembly of the Association of Yale Alumni on the Yale campus, attended by scores of Yale graduates, was devoted to Yale–New Haven relations under the title "On Common Ground." DiLieto in his remarks repeated what he had said on the day of his inauguration: "What is good for New Haven is good for Yale. And what is good for Yale is good for New Haven."

Much of this was admittedly symbolic. In the view of many urban activists both within and without Yale, it was nothing more than a smoke screen for Yale's continued adamant refusal to make voluntary payments in lieu of taxes on its tax-exempt properties.

The emphasis on finances in the relations between Yale and New Haven reflected economic and demographic trends following World War II affecting many small eastern cities: relocation of old-line manufacturers to areas with lower labor costs; a drop in population, especially among immigrant ethnic groups, increasingly replaced by minorities demanding greater public services; and, following the coming to power of the Nixon administration in 1969, the phasing out of aid directed to cities under the programs of Johnson's Great Society. All these factors placed a heavy burden on tax revenues, provided almost exclusively by real estate taxes, and thus directed political scrutiny to Yale, the value of whose tax-exempt real estate in New Haven amounted to a substantial percentage of the value of the entire property list.

During the last years of the Brewster administration, the city under Mayor Bartholomew Guida confronted Yale directly on the issue of its tax-exempt property. We have seen that New Haven was successful in 1973 in scuttling the university's plan for two new residential colleges to be built on previously taxable property, though ultimately the ordinance requiring permission to build the colleges had been declared illegal. At about the same time the city tried to place on the tax rolls a building occupied by Yale University Press, but the initiative failed. In a lawsuit contesting the denial of the tax exemption, Yale won a sweeping victory that reaffirmed the exemption for all of its noncommercial properties whether or not used for educational purposes.

Thus when Giamatti became president, Yale was legally secure in its property tax exemption, and it did not budge an inch. The university contributed more than its fair share to New Haven, Yale argued, through the pro bono activities and commercial patronage of its students, faculty, and staff, and as the city's largest employer and purchaser of goods and services. Giamatti was entirely comfortable with this posture. He was philosophically opposed to the expenditure of university funds to meet municipal needs. Even if he had been sympathetic,

Yale could not afford it. Yale would continue to use its good offices to promote private investment in development projects in New Haven, and would itself invest where considerations of safety and an adequate financial return were satisfied. But no more. The election of the nonconfrontational DiLieto in 1979 had taken the heat off, and low-decibel cooperation defined relations throughout the Giamatti years.

For all of the skepticism of urban activists (some of whom never forgave Giamatti for his position on the tax issue), symbolism and a sense of cultural affinity are extremely important in town-gown relations—and very hard to come by. Giamatti took advantage of his Italian and New Haven background to make a contribution in these respects that no prior Yale president could make. The university's tangible contributions to New Haven under its current administration, committed to helping the city and possessing the resources to carry out the commitment, are on a scale unimaginable in Giamatti's time (though they still do not include payments in lieu of taxes). But it was Giamatti who turned the university's human face to the city, and gave Yale a base of acceptance to build on.

The Labor Crisis

L abor relations at Yale in 1978, when Giamatti became
president, were, as we have seen, unstable. The last of
the three long strikes in the 1970s by the custodial and
maintenance workers had ended only the day before Giamatti's
appointment was announced, and the union's feisty business
manager, Vincent J. Sirabella, an in-your-face labor negotiator
of the old school, who had led the union through these strikes,
was already predicting a new strike when the 1977 contract
expired in 1980.

But in the spring of 1979 Sirabella resigned and was replaced by John W. Wilhelm, a thirty-five-year-old Yale graduate, who brought to his new job all of Sirabella's toughness but
had a far more sophisticated grasp of labor-management issues
than his predecessor. When in 1980 Yale and the union agreed
on a contract running until 1982 without a strike, amid public
declarations of a new climate of mutual respect and cooperation, there was every reason to hope that the university's long
period of labor instability was over. This hope was strength-
ened in 1982, when another contract was successfully negoti-

ated, extending until 1985. But it was not to be; the worst was still to come.

While Yale's custodial and maintenance workers had been unionized since the late 1960s, its white-collar workers—the clerical and technical personnel—were not represented by a union when Wilhelm came on the scene. On more than one occasion attempts to unionize them had failed. In the spring of 1971, while Yale's employee relations team was preoccupied with a strike of the custodial and maintenance workers, a group called the Yale Non-Faculty Action Committee had managed to gather the signatures of the necessary percentage of white-collar workers to force an election to determine whether a union would be certified to represent them. But when the vote came in the fall, after an organized campaign by Yale in opposition, the union was overwhelmingly rejected by a 70 percent majority, despite a 90 percent turnout of eligible voters. When in 1977 the white-collar workers again forced an election, it too was defeated, though by a reduced majority of 55 percent.

The arguments that Yale put forward to defeat unionization reflected a long tradition of paternalism toward white-collar workers, many of them wives and relatives of faculty and students encouraged to think of themselves as part of the educational enterprise. Clerical and technical workers "don't work at Yale," said the director of employee relations in 1971, "they work with Yale. Each person has a unique and personal relationship with the University." A letter to employees sounded the same theme: "A university is a special form of community with an unusual interdependence on a person-to-person level between those that are a part of it. . . . Education . . . remains a personal affair, and the sharing of pride in a worthwhile goal creates a spirit quite different than is usually observed in business or industry." A white-collar job at Yale was represented as a privilege. In keeping with this image Yale spokesmen stressed the comfortable working conditions and liberal vacation and sick-leave policies that the university offered its white-collar workers, and the close informal relationships most developed with their supervisors.

But in the matter of wages, white-collar workers lagged seriously behind. A 1976 study showed that almost half of them earned less than the minimum paid to the unionized custodial and maintenance workers. Women were discriminated against in both categories of workers, but this circumstance was more prejudicial to female white-collar workers, who made up some 80 percent of that category, contrasted with about one-third of the blue-collar workers. A study commissioned by the university after the 1977 union election revealed that while the overwhelming majority of white-collar workers liked their work, 65 percent thought it "extremely urgent" to improve salary levels, and another 20 percent thought it "urgent." These concerns were undoubtedly reflected in the relative narrowness of the 1977 vote compared with that of 1971. Yale knew that the problem of white-collar salaries had to be addressed, and over a three-year period beginning in 1980 it made salary adjustments in that category aggregating more than 30 percent, well in excess of inflation. But it could not respond quickly enough to avoid a renewed threat of unionization.

The failure by unions at Yale in the 1970s in organizing its white-collar workers reflected a national condition. By the early 1980s barely 15 percent of office workers in America were unionized, probably even fewer in colleges and universities, where the argument that unionism had no place for those who were privileged to participate in the educational enterprise had strong appeal. But other trends were now at work. The growing women's movement was asserting that women were entitled to pay equal to men's for comparable work, an argument with particular force among Yale's predominantly female clerical and technical workers. The civil rights movement was also a factor: some 15 percent of the white-collar workers at Yale were now members of minorities. John Wilhelm believed that he could create a precedent with national implications by unionizing Yale's white-collar workers and negotiating for them a contract that went far toward eliminating the discrimination in wage levels that they had historically experienced compared with other categories of workers. It was time for the labor movement to start paying attention to white-collar workers, he said, for "the issues that women workers have—which largely involve taking control of their work lives—are very susceptible to being addressed by unions." So in 1981 John Wilhelm announced that a new union under his leadership, Local 34 of the Federation of University Employees, AFL-CIO, would seek to be certified by the National Labor Relations Board to represent Yale's clerical and technical workers in contract negotiations.

Organizing activities began in the spring of 1981 but proceeded slowly until the following spring, when negotiation of the extension of the contract with the custodial and maintenance union had been completed and Wilhelm could give the matter his full attention. Workers were asked to sign cards petitioning for an election, and by the fall of 1982 Wilhelm was predicting publicly that an election would take place before the end of the academic year. In January 1983 the union filed with the National Labor Relations Board cards signed by more than 1,500 white-collar workers, substantially more than half of those eligible to be represented, far above the 30 percent threshold established by law. After hearings throughout the spring to resolve disputes between Yale and the union over the class of employees eligible to vote, an election was ordered to take place on May 18.

An employee who signs a card requesting a certification

election is not obligated to vote in favor of certifying the union to represent the employees, and Yale mounted a spirited defense of the status quo. The campaign largely took the form of fliers entitled "Another Viewpoint," distributed in several editions over the spring of 1983, supplemented by two longer Election Fact Books distributed in April and May, emphasizing a variation of the familiar paternalistic message of past campaigns: "In an institution as varied and diverse as Yale where value is placed on individual skill and merit, the uniform requirements and procedural formalities imposed by a union contract would discourage individual initiative and stifle recognition of merit." A hotline to respond to questions was also provided.

Personal campaigning by Yale spokesmen was not part of the effort. Giamatti, ever the enemy of "coercion" in the "free and ordered space" of the university, vetoed such campaigning, perhaps in response to a richly cynical "Invitation to the Yale Administration," published by the union in the campus newspaper under the heading "At Yale, We Can Do Better." It called for the elimination of "captive audience" meetings and urged instead, in the quoted words of a Yale spokesman, "civilized debate, grounded on the facts and based on the record, in keeping with the collegial spirit that animates the University." There were a few impersonal open meetings during lunch hours conducted by the personnel department, but little else in the way of personal contact. Employees were to be left free to make up their minds on the basis of written materials furnished to them or deposited at "reading centers" throughout the university, free from the pressure of face-to-face persuasion.

When the vote came, 1,267 workers voted in favor of representation by Local 34 and 1,228 voted against, a margin of 39 votes. The turnout was 94 percent. Yale had at last to deal with a unionized body of clerical and technical workers. Many at

Yale thought the outcome would have been different if Yale had campaigned more aggressively, sending its representatives, perhaps even the charismatic president himself, to meet with the workers in small groups and argue the university's position. It is true that coercion has no rightful place in a certification election; it is in fact unlawful. But "coercion" in the language of labor relations is what lawyers call a term of art, its meaning different in a legal context than in common parlance. The expressing of views, argument, or opinion in an election setting is not "coercion" so long as, in the words of the applicable statute, "such expression contains no threat of reprisal or force or promise of benefit." Meetings of Yale representatives with groups of white-collar employees under controlled conditions, even during working hours, would have been considered by most managers an entirely proper defensive tactic. Giamatti, with his fear of undue pressure and the academic's confidence in the efficacy of the written word to convey an argument, even to a nonacademic audience, evidently considered forgoing such meetings to be the principled course. To others it seemed merely naïve.

The summer of 1983 was spent by the union in developing its initial position. Collective bargaining sessions began in October. The fall months were devoted to nonsalary issues. The union submitted its first salary proposal in December. It called for a 25 percent across-the-board salary increase on February 1, 1984, and other salary adjustments that the university calculated would result in a wage increase of some 56 percent over the first seventeen months of the contract. This was surely posturing, but it established a goal that the union never abandoned: eliminating or drastically narrowing over the life of the contract the discrimination in wage levels that Yale's white-collar workers had historically experienced compared with other categories of workers. Yale's initial proposal of 4½ percent increases on July 1 of each of the next three years, while less than the university must have known it would eventually have to pay, similarly signaled its position: Yale would continue to do what it could to increase the compensation of its white-collar workers, but there were other constituencies that its budget had to accommodate—faculty, whose salaries had lagged behind other employees in the bad 1970s; students, affected by rising tuition levels and the reduced availability of financial aid; other employees. "This dispute is not about money," said Yale's principal negotiator in response to the union's assertion that Yale could afford to meet its demands; "it's about priorities." Yale's provost, William C. Brainard, made a more candid, if impolitic, remark, widely exploited by the union: "I know that one can't live the way one would like to, or the way one would like one's family to live, on a Yale clerical and technical salary. That's a national problem, which Yale can't be expected to solve."

With so great a gulf separating the two sides, it was no surprise that by the spring no settlement was in sight, and the union voted to strike in the first week of April. Horrified at the prospect of a strike during the period of final examinations, commencement, and reunions, Giamatti, without adequate consultation, struck a deal with Wilhelm: Yale would enter into an agreement with the union covering all of the nonsalary issues that had been settled. The wage issue would be left open for later settlement. The union would not strike in the spring, but it would reserve the right to do so later if an impasse were reached on the wage issue.

The interim agreement obligated Yale to put into effect immediately some changes in working conditions that had so far been conceded to the union only conditionally, pending agreement on all contract issues. Such an arrangement, though highly unusual in a labor contract negotiation, might not have been seriously prejudicial to Yale if the changes had not represented major concessions. But in order to avert a strike—only temporarily, as it turned out—Giamatti consented to the inclusion in the interim agreement of a provision guaranteeing to Local 34 a modified union-shop clause in the final contract.

The union shop—the recognition by an employer of the union's right to require that every employee pay union dues as a condition of employment—is of vital importance to a union negotiating its first contract, because it assures the flow of money into the union treasury without which the union cannot survive. For that reason the conventional wisdom in labor negotiations is that a union shop is conceded, if at all, only at the very end, when it is a powerful weapon in persuading the union to moderate its financial demands. By giving up that weapon without reaching agreement on the wage issue, Giamatti, a neophyte in labor negotiations, left Yale seriously weakened when the most difficult contract issues had to be settled.

Continued negotiations over the summer of 1984 did not come close to producing a settlement on the central issue of wages. By late September, Yale had improved its offer to provide for across-the-board annual increases of 6.5 percent, 5.3 percent, and 5.3 percent over the three years of the contract, which, when added to various other adjustments, resulted in an overall increase in wage levels by the end of the contract that Yale calculated at 24.2 percent. The union was demanding across-the-board increases of 9 percent, 10 percent and 10 percent as part of a package which, again as calculated by Yale, would increase wage levels by the end of the contract by 57.5 percent. These were obviously very big differences, and on September 26, 1984, the union commenced a strike. By the time it had ended nearly four months later, it had imposed great stress on the university and taken a dreadful personal toll on its president.

Part of the pressure on Giamatti was inherent in his position as chief executive officer of an institution under siege. But the pressure was enormously intensified by Wilhelm's strategy of personalizing the dispute, of making the strike Giamatti's strike. Giamatti's own expressions of his commitment to civilized discourse and fair play were quoted over and over again in the union's literature. As we saw, this tactic was employed in the "Invitation to the Yale Administration" to refrain from holding personal meetings with employees during the certification election campaign; the university officer quoted in that statement was not Giamatti himself, but it might have been, for the remark perfectly expressed his own sentiments: "Yale hopes to promote a civilized debate, grounded on the facts and based on the record, in keeping with the collegial spirit that animates the University." The appeal to Giamatti's respect for civility and fair play seems to have had two purposes. The first and obvious one was to encourage him to moderate the university's position. The "Invitation" may in fact have had that effect, for as we have seen, Yale did refrain from holding personal meetings with employees during the certification election. During the strike itself, this purpose was less clearly served. Appeals to Giamatti's principles seem almost to have stiffened his resolve.

The second purpose for emphasizing Giamatti's respect for civility and fair play was less honorable. It was to provide a basis, when he did not accede to the union's demands, for portraying him as a hypocrite. The sensitive Giamatti was extremely vulnerable to this tactic. We hear the pain in one of his communications to the Yale community during the election campaign:

> The most troubling note during the last few weeks has been the assertion by some that Yale and I do not value and respect clerical and technical individuals and their work. . . . I find this assertion profoundly troubling. One of the most impor-

tant values I hold, and one that I have repeated and acted on since 1978, is my belief in the essential need in our University for mutual respect and a sense of the dignity of the individual as we pursue our common goal. Lest there be any doubt, let me say it again. This University cares deeply about the value of each individual and about the work and personal dignity of every member of this community.

Ironically, Giamatti's reassertion of his values served to reinforce the image of him fostered by the union, and left him more vulnerable to further suggestions of hypocrisy.

The union tactic of building Giamatti up in order to tear him down continued into the strike itself. The form of informational flier used by the union throughout the strike to communicate its position was headed by Giamatti's own words after the election: "It is now time for us to put aside our differences and in good faith to work together." Against this quotation, the title of the flier, "In Good Faith," seemed almost a taunt. It is to be contrasted with the constant verbal abuse heaped upon Giamatti by union pickets wherever he went in New Haven, combined with the threat of physical intimidation that was often present—he was certainly jostled and spat upon on more than one occasion. Some sense of the harassment he was constantly subjected to can be conveyed by an excerpt from one of the songs contained in the Local 34 Song Book distributed to picketing workers to provide ammunition for torturing Giamatti the hypocrite:

> It is Bart who hires the lawyers, it is Bart who calls the shots;
> He treats his women workers like a bunch of timid tots.
> It is Bartlett who has tied the university in knots,
> But the union makes us strong.

Giamatti, who had been appalled at the demonstrations and sloganeering of the sixties, now saw them repeated, this time directed specifically at him.

The pain inflicted on the sensitive Giamatti by these accusations was intensified by growing dissatisfaction with the
conduct of the strike within the faculty, whose respect for and
loyalty to Giamatti had long been his pride and strength. Of
course, in a politically liberal institution like Yale it was to be
expected that many faculty members would instinctively side
with the workers in any labor dispute, though the level of vi-
tuperation aimed at Giamatti in faculty meetings by some of
the union's rabid supporters startled many of their colleagues.
But as the strike dragged on, more moderate elements grew
impatient. Particularly galling to the besieged president must
have been the remarks of the respected Yale historian Gaddis
Smith, who was no fire-eater, at a so-called Rally for Reconciliation in mid-November:

> When people fail to solve a common problem and turn to
> conflict, they have a most unfortunate habit of thinking more
> about the defeat of the other side than about the mutual
> interest both sides have in a harmonious settlement. . . . We
> see [this] to some degree in the strike at Yale. . . . As such
> attitudes intensify, both sides, in this as in any dispute, begin
> to measure progress in terms of the pain suffered by the other
> side. . . . When two sides become locked in such stubborn and
> negative positions, the ultimate outcome will not be a settle-
> ment—but a capitulation. One side can claim "victory," but
> the larger community of which both are a part will have suf-
> fered defeat—and the cost will be borne by all through years of
> bitterness, ill feeling, and memories of which we are not
> proud.

Smith was a near contemporary of Giamatti and, like him, a
rising star on the Yale faculty in the 1960s and 1970s. Some
people believed that when Kingman Brewster left the presidency, Smith, too, had aspired to succeed him. Giamatti, ever
sensitive to criticism, must have deeply resented the charge of
stubbornness from his old rival for conduct he felt was in de-

fense of an important budgetary principle—the more so, perhaps, because there was surely at least a grain of truth in what
Smith said.

Negotiations, which had been virtually suspended since
early October, were resumed in mid-November, and when they
did not produce an agreement, the union announced that its
members would return to work during the holiday season,
threatening resumption of the strike in January if there was no
settlement. The holidays provided a cooling-off period, during
which it must have become clear to both sides that the time
had come to settle. And so on January 21, 1985, before the strike
was resumed, agreement was finally reached.

Who "won"? There can be no question that the final settlement obligated Yale to pay to its white-collar workers over the
three-year contract period and beyond far more than it had
originally offered or expected to pay. But comparison of the
final settlement with the respective proposals of the two sides
before the holidays suggests that both Yale and the union
achieved important objectives. In a compensation package with
so many parts and so many variables, accurate conclusions are
difficult to draw. But an analysis of the reconciliation of the
respective proposals for across-the-board salary increases is
instructive. In November, Yale had offered a three-year contract beginning, retroactively, on July 1, 1984, and running until
July 1, 1987, with annual salary increments of 6.5 percent, 5.6
percent, and 5.0 percent. The union proposal called for annual
increments of 8 percent over the same period. The final settlement incorporated Yale's proposal for the first year, ending July
1, 1985, but pushed the contract out for thirty-one months from
that date to January 31, 1988, with two salary increments of 6.5
percent and 7.25 percent, each to take effect in two steps at
approximately equal intervals. Extending the term of the contract and implementing the salary increments in steps saved

Yale money over the contract term and permitted it to claim that the final settlement was "within the financial limits of the University which were identified to the Union last fall," notwithstanding the greater percentage salary increments than it had previously offered. The greater increments, on the other hand, served Wilhelm's objective of lifting the level of wages at the end of the contract, from which future contract negotiations would start. Yale might, in short, be paying out no more dollars over the life of the contract than it had offered before the holidays, but future contracts would be more costly.

Can the unwillingness of Yale to settle the strike earlier be fairly laid at the feet of a stubborn, emotional, and thus unreasonable, president? Many of Giamatti's critics certainly thought and said so. But the relative merits of the positions of labor and management are seldom clear in a contentious dispute that both parties believe to have far-reaching consequences. A dispassionate observer must conclude that the case against Giamatti is not proved.

The 1984 strike was seriously disruptive at Yale, and the final settlement was expensive. The inevitable adjustment of the low wage levels of white-collar workers had now to be made more quickly than Yale wished, and the settlement undoubtedly caused some reordering of budget priorities well into the future, just as the university had said it would. But it was hardly the end of the world. Yale continued to balance its budgets after the strike, and life went on.

For Giamatti himself the consequences of the strike were far more serious and lasting. A divisive strike, during which the issues inevitably become personalized, is very hard on any executive, however thick his skin. But Giamatti's fundamental values had been assailed. When he repeatedly insisted on the importance of the clerical and technical employees and their work and asserted the need for mutual respect and the dignity of the individual, he was not merely echoing the old paternalistic line that Yale and other universities had used to defend against aggressive unionism. These sentiments reflected his deepest beliefs of what a university should be. When challenges to his sincerity were accompanied by tactics of confrontation and sloganeering, which were anathema to him, the hurt was compounded. And when, finally, he sensed that he was losing the support of moderates in his own faculty and (though never expressed publicly) some members of the Yale Corporation, it became nearly unbearable.

It must, alas, be said that Giamatti was poorly suited by experience and temperament to confront so great a crisis as the 1984 labor dispute. It left him a weary, angry, and disillusioned man, aged beyond his years, the "cinder" he himself had feared he might become. Giamatti's handling of the crisis did not permanently harm Yale. The harm was to Giamatti himself.

Resignation

On April 22, 1985, Giamatti announced that he would leave the presidency of Yale at the end of the 1985–86 academic year. It was not a spur-of-the-moment decision. He had intended to leave a year earlier in happier times, but the uncertain labor situation had caused him to postpone his departure. Now he was exhausted and disillusioned by the strike and by what he believed had been tepid support for his management of it from some elements of the university community. He had, he said, "done what I can do" to accomplish his goals. All the proprieties were observed at the press conference that followed his announcement. The Yale Corporation expressed "profound regret" at his decision. "The Corporation," said its senior fellow J. Richardson Dilworth, "regards President Giamatti's term of office as very successful in every conceivable sense." There had certainly been no pressure on Giamatti to resign, but he knew the strike had cooled his relationship with some members of the Corporation. He was hurt and unhappy, and he intended to leave Yale at the end of his presidency.

As a faculty member, and even as president, where his salary had barely reached six figures, Giamatti had accumulated no savings, and he wanted to earn some money to provide for his family's security. He believed he could realize that objective by becoming an executive in corporate America. He turned for help in identifying and evaluating opportunities to a small group of acquaintances prominent in the corporate community. Principal among these was Fay Vincent, whom Giamatti had met some years earlier when Vincent was the chief executive officer of Columbia Pictures. They had been introduced by a mutual friend, Peter Knipe, a Yale College classmate of Giamatti and a Yale Law School classmate of Vincent, who thought that two young presidents of the same age, one of a successful business and the other of a prominent university, both with Yale connections, should know each other. The introductory dinner at Knipe's house in Princeton was a success—Giamatti was verbally bested for once when Vincent capped off a debate as to whether Columbia Pictures or Yale was easier to manage by asserting that Yale must be easier since an English teacher could do it—and the two men became fast friends, socializing regularly—over dinners in New Haven's Italian neighborhood, at Yale football games, at gatherings of Vincent's business associates in New York.

In 1985 Vincent was executive vice president of Coca-Cola, which had bought Columbia Pictures, and he had wide contacts among corporate executives. He called many of them on Giamatti's behalf, and interviews were arranged and held, but nothing came of it. Giamatti was very disappointed. So was Vincent, who was distressed to discover that none of his friends among chief executive officers of large companies had the imagination to see what a man of Giamatti's stature and talents could offer as an executive in charge of public issues, the corporate ambassador to the outside world.

From the time of the announcement that he was leaving the

presidency, many of Giamatti's colleagues had urged him to return to teaching. He was now resigned to doing so—against the advice of Vincent, who said that the charismatic Giamatti on the faculty would be like Pavarotti in the chorus, singing too loud even if he did not intend to. Then, unexpectedly, an alternative presented itself. It will be recalled that when Giamatti's name appeared on the list of possible candidates for the Yale presidency in 1977, he had said that the only thing he ever wanted to be president of was the American League. An alert Bud Selig, owner of baseball's Milwaukee Brewers, playing a major role in the selection of a new commissioner of baseball in 1984, remembered that Yale's president was a baseball fan, and asked him whether he would like to be considered a candidate for the job. Yale's labor difficulties of that year were already in the offing, and it was not a good time. But now, in 1986, the position of president of the National League was about to become available, and it was offered to Giamatti.

He hesitated. True, the job would pay him an attractive multiple of his Yale salary. But it did not carry heavy responsibilities beyond public relations and the supervision of National League umpires. Giamatti was afraid he would be bored. Again he consulted Fay Vincent, who urged him to take it. The salary was right, and the job's light duties would afford him an opportunity to speak and write and, above all, get some exercise and pay some attention to his health, which his friends worried about even if he didn't. And so he took it, the appointment to become effective at the end of 1986.

Between the time that Giamatti announced his retirement and the date of his departure a full academic year at Yale was to pass, and we must pause to consider the major issue at the university during that year—unrest arising from Yale's policy of retaining in its endowment portfolio the stock of companies doing business in South Africa—and its effect on the lame-duck president.

In the years before Giamatti's presidency, Yale's policy with respect to the exercise of social responsibility in the management of its endowment was contained in a set of guidelines that grew out of a series of meetings of various university constituencies held in the late 1960s. These guidelines were set forth and explained in a volume published in 1972 by Yale University Press entitled *The Ethical Investor,* which asserted, as a "moral minimum" of corporate conduct, an obligation not to impose social injury, defined as "activities which violate, or frustrate the enforcement of, rules of domestic or international law intended to protect individuals against deprivation of health, safety or basic freedoms." And it also asserted that it is the duty of every shareholder, including universities, to take such action as it can to prevent social injury by corporations in which it invests.

This duty is discharged when the shareholder exercises every power at its disposal, including communicating with the management, voting on shareholder proposals, and even voting to change the management, to bring about the correction of offending corporate practices. But divestment was not called for "unless these practices are grave and unless all methods of correcting them have failed or appear doomed to failure." The explanation of the guidelines is quite explicit on this point. "We have not recommended," it states,

> that divestment be employed as a first-line method for correcting corporate policies, for we think it improbable that it can have that effect. . . . And if divestment is not an effective technique, we see no other reason to recommend it. We have concluded that institutional decontamination—the quest for a clean portfolio—is not a supportable or even feasible goal

and that the institution which sells (or eschews) a security for that reason succeeds only in turning its back on controversy and possibly impairing its economic strength.

The guidelines set forth in *The Ethical Investor* remained the criteria for the exercise of social responsibility in the management of Yale's endowment, including investment in companies doing business in South Africa, until 1978, when Hanna Gray appointed an advisory committee on South African investments to reexamine the appropriateness of the existing criteria in that special case. Its report to the Yale Corporation included a recommendation that Yale divest itself of ownership of the securities of three categories of American companies that, in the committee's view, abetted the maintenance of apartheid: (1) banks that lend money to the government of South Africa; (2) companies that contribute significantly to the South African economy by participating in a strategic sector of the economy, making substantial loans to private businesses in South Africa, or deriving a significant portion of their revenues from South African operations; and (3) companies which decline to implement certain employment practices (the so-called Sullivan Principles, after the American cleric Leon Sullivan, a member of the board of directors of General Motors, who formulated them) designed to insure equal opportunity and treatment to nonwhite employees in the workplace. It would, the committee said, be "inappropriate for the University to be a part owner of such businesses, or to share in their profits."

These recommendations constituted a significant retreat (or advance, depending on one's point of view) from the rejection in the 1972 guidelines of "decontamination" of the portfolio as grounds for divestment, and the Yale Corporation declined to accept the recommendations in full. In the event that an Ameri-

can bank or company makes loans or otherwise engages in
activities of a special character that provide major assistance to
the South African government, or declines to implement the
Sullivan Principles, the Corporation announced, Yale will consider divestment, but only after taking into account whether it
would be "likely to impair the capacity of the University to carry
out its primary educational mission." This formulation, of
course, fell significantly short of the recommendations of the
committee, and far short of the wishes of those who believed
that Yale should divest itself of the securities of all companies
that do business of any kind in South Africa. It did result in
some changes in Yale's portfolio: in 1979 Yale sold its stock in
Morgan Guaranty Trust Company and Citicorp, lenders to the
government of South Africa. But other companies with extensive South African interests remained in the portfolio: IBM, for
example, which manufactured the computers through which
the apparatus of apartheid was implemented.

Thus matters stood at the beginning of the Giamatti presidency, and until 1984 activity on the issue was largely in abeyance. In that year, however, a newly formed student group
called the Coalition Against Apartheid (CAA) became the
channel for increasing student insistence on total divestment.
By the spring of 1985, the campuswide focus on the strike
having passed, signs of unrest began to appear. There was a
small student overnight vigil outside Woodbridge Hall, where
the president's office is located. And at graduation, many seniors accepted their degrees with black-wrapped forearms pro-
testing Yale's South African investment policies.

The following fall, at the beginning of Giamatti's last academic year as president, the CAA stepped up its activity, gaining the support of Yale's unions, always glad for an opportunity
to embarrass the university. The signatures of more than three
thousand students and faculty on a petition calling for total

divestment was presented to Giamatti. And the sloganeering, so offensive to him, began: "Hey, Giamatti, get off the potty," shouted picketers outside a New Haven hotel where Giamatti was making an appearance.

The Yale Corporation attempted to respond. In November it announced an unequivocal commitment to hold in its endowment only shares of companies which honored the Sullivan Principles, now much expanded from their original formulation, and which either "publicly demonstrate that they are actively working for the dismantlement of apartheid, or have a plan for the orderly withdrawal of their operations from South Africa." But the lines were by this time too clearly drawn for protestors to be satisfied by anything short of total and immediate divestment. And significantly, for the first time the Yale Corporation broke ranks: four of its members entered a public dissent from Corporation policy, urging total divestment. A further modest broadening of the circumstances in which Yale would divest its shares in certain companies, announced in March 1986, had no greater calming effect.

Matters came to a head in early April, when protestors erected wooden and aluminum shanties in Beinecke Plaza, a major Yale venue for large outdoor gatherings, setting in motion a series of demonstrations and confrontations eerily reminiscent of the sixties. Yale dithered, clumsily trying to find its rhythm by recourse to procedures, now rusty, developed almost twenty years earlier to deal with the unrest of Brewster's time. On the day the shanties were erected, a Friday, Giamatti told the protestors that they would have to be removed immediately, since permission to erect them had not been obtained in advance from the university. Later the same day, secretary John Wilkinson, the university officer authorized to give permission, said that the shanties could remain in place until the next day, when he would receive a delegation to seek permission retroactively. At that meeting, Wilkinson granted permission for the shanties to remain in place through the following Saturday, when a meeting of the Yale Corporation was scheduled in New Haven. After that meeting they would have to be removed.

On the Monday following the meeting of the Yale Corporation, the shanties were removed from Beinecke Plaza over the opposition of protestors, seventy-five of whom, mostly students, were arrested and charged with trespass when they refused police orders to leave. This confrontation led to a series of demonstrations in support of those arrested, each involving several hundred students. On one occasion, as Giamatti was leaving Woodbridge Hall, he was shoved and knocked off his feet by a student protestor. The shove was probably unintentional, but Giamatti, always sensitive about the unsteadiness resulting from the congenital muscular weakness in his lower legs, was not so sure, and he threatened to have the student expelled. Cooler heads eventually prevailed.

But if what he thought was physical intimidation annoyed Giamatti, the persistence of sloganeering offended him even more. The week before, when John Wilkinson had ordered the removal of a large wooden structure built in Beinecke Plaza as a "memorial" to blacks who had died as a result of recent unrest in South Africa, a group of protestors had followed him home chanting, "Wilkinson, you can't hide! You support genocide!" Now the slogan of choice was "Hey, hey, ho, ho, there's blood on your portfolio." Said an exasperated Giamatti, "If people haven't discovered at this late date, since the sixties, that standing around and yelling at people is not the way to get them to change their minds, they're never going to learn it. . . . In a university, discourse takes place, not shouting." It must have seemed to him that the homilies defining the university as a "free and ordered space" and his repeated insistence on the "awesome power" of language as "the medium in which the race lives" had fallen on deaf ears.

As a final affront, a faculty committee appointed by Giamatti to consider the best use of Beinecke Plaza for the rest of the school year concluded that the shanties should be rebuilt there and remain through graduation. The president was to have before him until his last day on the job a visible reminder of the violation of his highest ideals for the university. For him it was the ultimate betrayal. For others the confrontation at Beinecke Plaza, coming as it did so soon after the 1984 strike, was further confirmation that Giamatti's presidency was fatally flawed by his inability to function well in an environment of turmoil.

An Appraisal

As a teacher and scholar Giamatti was universally admired, and as a baseball executive in his career after Yale nearly so. But the reviews are mixed on his performance as president of Yale. It is generally thought that the respect and affection of his faculty colleagues and the New Haven community made it possible for him to succeed in the important areas of budget reform and town-gown relations. And no one disputes his success in setting forth a vision, rooted in his knowledge of and admiration for the values of the English Renaissance, of the nature of a university and the purpose of a liberal education. But in other respects, particularly his handling of contentious matters—labor relations and student unrest—he has been widely criticized. Gaddis Smith, Yale's distinguished emeritus professor of history, whose study of Yale in the twentieth century is soon to be published, has called his presidency "disastrous," the inevitable consequence of his "confrontational style and psychological fragility." For his critics the prolonged and bitter 1984 strike of the university's white-collar workers became the symbol of Giamatti's failure. His old friend and faculty colleague Alvin Kernan thought that it had "destroyed his presidency." Whether or not that is true, we have seen that it nearly destroyed him personally. The weary and disillusioned man who left Yale in the aftermath of the strike reminded some of Masaccio's *Expulsion of Adam and Eve* in Florence's Brancacci Chapel, retreating, chastised and humiliated, from the Garden of Eden, Giamatti's symbol for the free and ordered space he believed Yale should be.

Professor Smith writes of Giamatti's "confrontational style." This seems extreme. It is true that Giamatti was less inclined to avoid confrontation than was Kingman Brewster, who had skillfully forestalled it when he could, and steered personally clear of it when he could not. Professor Smith may have had in mind Giamatti's angry overreaction when he was knocked off his feet in the confusion of a student rally against Yale's investment policies in the final days of his presidency. This incident had a particular resonance for Professor Smith, because the student Giamatti held responsible was a member of Pierson College, of which Smith was at the time the master. But it is hard to think of any occasion on which Giamatti provoked confrontation, certainly never physical confrontation. Perhaps Professor Smith means to include as confrontational Giamatti's frequently expressed disapproval of the sloganeering and implied threats of violence that went with the labor and student unrest of the time.

He is on firmer ground when he writes of Giamatti's "psychological fragility." We have seen that from his early days Bart Giamatti was high-strung and sensitive to criticism. The insecurity that these outward signs suggested led him on occasion to withdraw defensively into himself, to become moody, testy, secretive. Those who worked with him closely sometimes experienced this darker side. "Giamatti doesn't walk on water," his close friend John Wilkinson observed. "He can be tempestuous, difficult, cranky." Sam Chauncey, a veteran of the Brewster years carrying over briefly into the Giamatti administration as secretary of the university, recalled sitting in Giamatti's living room, "Bart yelling and screaming" at the provost, and his wife Toni on the stairway landing crying. "These are my memories of working for Bart. Agony."

Temper. And impatience. This latter defect lay behind what many felt was his tendency to micromanage. One of his deans recalls that he was often in the background silently duplicating work he had assigned to be sure it was "done right." He was chronically guilty of failing to consult colleagues, and of not keeping them "in the loop." We have seen that inadequate consultation led to unwise decisions during the 1984 labor dispute. Even where there were not costly mistakes, there were frustrations—and occasionally defections. Peter Halsey, for one, the university's valued emissary to state and local government, finally left when he was embarrassed to learn that the position of the university he was putting forth before a legislative committee had been superseded by a Giamatti decision, made privately after consultation with another colleague, of which he had not been informed.

All of these deficiencies in the quality of Giamatti's leadership may perhaps be classified under the rubric "psychological fragility." The strike was certainly a nightmare for an impatient micromanager, an event he could neither control nor bring to a satisfactory end. But Professor Smith is surely suggesting something different and more basic: Giamatti's inability to accept with equanimity the discontinuities between the real world as it is and the ideal world as it ought to be, to absorb disappointment with the conduct of others in a spirit of tolerance, the "mingling of acceptance and regret" that he so prized in Ariosto. This is the flaw that repeatedly created such mental anguish for Giamatti. For those who loved and admired him, the result was classical tragedy. For many others, it was simply failure; for some, "disastrous" failure.

There were elements of the 1984 strike which help to explain why it so dramatically revealed Giamatti's vulnerability. In his memoir *In Plato's Cave*, Alvin Kernan says that Giamatti "destroyed his presidency" by exercising his "old-fashioned sense of his responsibilities" and accepting a long strike by Yale's clerical and technical workers rather than meet wage demands he didn't believe Yale could afford. The picture is of a conscientious administrator of the old school holding to the "right" course regardless of practical consequences. This is certainly accurate as far as it goes, but the whole truth requires further elaboration.

Elsewhere Kernan speaks more generally: Giamatti, he writes, was "the last hurrah of the old type of college president, more a scholar than a bureaucrat, and his story is a tragic one of how the old ways came to grief in the new university." As this assessment suggests, the fundamental reason for Giamatti's vulnerability lay in the nature of the place Yale had become by the 1980s. Earlier in his book, Kernan explains what he means by "the new university." During the late twentieth century, he says, the elitist model of the university that had theretofore prevailed was "displaced by a type of education . . . institutionalizing the democratic values of American society." Symptomatic of the change was the rejection by students of the "upper-middle-class social ethos that had governed the older educational institutions," including the principle of hierarchy, the traditional master-apprentice relationship between faculty and students. The most dramatic evidences of all this were the protests and demonstrations against authority of all kinds in the 1960s and 1970s. At the same time, Kernan adds, "where the old university had tried to be an ivory tower of unbiased knowledge, outside and above politics, teaching and research now were politicized and treated as instruments of popular reform." A natural result was activism of many faculty members in political issues affecting the campus.

Giamatti was deeply out of sympathy with most of the values of the "new university" and their manifestations. He respected the principle of hierarchy. As a teacher, though always respectful of his students, he was at pains to arrange his classroom and conduct his classes in such a way as to establish the primacy of the master. He thought that members of the faculty abandoned the principle when, allowing their private sentiments to overcome what he believed to be their institutional responsibilities, they openly joined with students in championing political causes. And, of course, he was appalled by student and labor demonstrations, with their threat of violence and shouted slogans—"language mediated through the bullhorn." The ideal university, he believed, must be a "free and ordered space," where issues are resolved after rational and civilized dialogue.

The 1984 strike was in part an expression of the values of the "new university," for it unexpectedly demonstrated that one of the principal features of the new order, the weakening of the principle of hierarchy, could also be present in labor relations. We have seen that the defining pattern of Yale's relationship with its white-collar workers before the strike was a paternalistic hierarchy, in which each worker was thought to have a personal—though clearly subordinate—status in the university's common educational enterprise. Giamatti must have understood intellectually that this pattern was now a relic of an earlier time. But his whole life had been spent in academic environments where it was taken for granted, and it was distressing to him to see it unceremoniously dumped without a rational dialogue. What had become of the "mutual respect"

and "sense of the dignity of the individual as we pursue
our common goal" that he had insisted on in his communications to employees during the 1984 labor dispute? The reality
of Yale's relations with its white-collar workers was not the
cooperative hierarchy he had idealized. He was hurt by this
realization.

Giamatti's respect for hierarchy was further offended by
the open intervention of many faculty members on the side of
the strikers and the students who rallied on their behalf. His
colleagues had betrayed their obligation to the university and
personally let him down. And as we have seen, the abusive
conduct of the strikers and their supporters, much of it directed at Giamatti personally, immeasurably intensified his de-
spair. When the strike was over, every reasonable observer
knew that life would go on, that Yale's finances and morale
would in time recover. But how could a leader so plainly and
deeply wounded by the event be thought of as anything but a
failure?

From the vantage point of early 1985, especially after Giamatti had announced his resignation in April, the admirers of
Kingman Brewster—and there were many, some of whom had
never accepted Giamatti as a worthy successor—looked back
on what they remembered as Camelot's golden age. Where was
Brewster's capacity for managing conflict, so indispensable in
the modern "multiversity," with its naturally warring constituencies? What had happened to Brewster's emphasis in building
up the sciences and the graduate schools? Had Giamatti's improved relationship with New Haven been anything but talk?
What about the curriculum reform that Giamatti had championed as a faculty member, the need to tighten the loosely
structured "distributional guidelines" instituted in the sixties,
"so lacking in force," he had said, "that they could not guide a

vulture to month-old carrion, much less a freshman to self-education"? Here, surely, was the end of a failed presidency.

This negative verdict on Giamatti's performance as Yale's president was widespread within the university, but it was by no means universal: it would be an exaggeration to conclude that he had lost the respect and support of most of Yale's faculty and administration. Nearly everyone would have agreed that Giamatti lacked Brewster's adaptability—the quality that justified Brewster in observing privately that Yale had survived his tenure because the knaves were not smart and the smart were not knaves. Most would have subscribed to the verdict of Law School dean Guido Calabresi, a friend and admirer of Giamatti's, that "Bart would have had a hard time being president in 1969–70. I don't think he would have been flexible enough to survive." The personal toll the presidency exacted on Giamatti was obvious in the startling physical change from the slim young prince to a much older man, gray and growing paunchy; but most observers looked upon the change with charitable sadness rather than judgmental blame. And few people had had occasion to experience his temper and impatience. By and large the Yale community, unaware of how disillusioned he was, still saw in Giamatti the charismatic scholar-teacher they had always known.

Nostalgia for Brewster was tempered, too, by a general recognition that the pervasive reality of the Giamatti years was a budget crisis, and that fairness required that his limited achievements in some areas be evaluated in that light. There seems no reason to believe that Giamatti would have neglected the sciences if money had been plentiful. When he became president in 1978, nearly two decades had passed since C. P. Snow famously divided the academic world into the scientists, with "the future in their bones," and the "literary intellectuals" (as Snow dismissively called them), rooted in the past, "tone deaf" to science and wishing that "the future did not exist." It was no longer necessary to choose sides, and Giamatti did not. In his homily to incoming freshmen in 1979, dealing with the sciences at Yale and entitled "Nature Justly Viewed," he said, "There is a common fallacy of educational thinking that a liberal education is synonymous with the humanities. Nothing could be further from the truth. A liberally educated mind is precisely one that has composed itself sufficiently to . . . find the same satisfaction in applying the results of technological experiments as in applying any other kind of knowledge, for the betterment of human kind." Nor was Giamatti indifferent to the individual research activities of Yale's scientific faculty. His administration worked hard with them to find accommodation between the university's interest in the public dissemination of the results of their research and the legitimate interest of commercial sponsors in the right to exclusive use of what they have paid for; and to resist intrusive overregulation by the federal government of all university activities as a condition of financial support for specific research.

Within the financial constraints to which he was subject, Giamatti took concrete steps to demonstrate his commitment to the sciences. In 1985 he persuaded a reluctant Sidney Altman, the young chairman of the biology department, to take time away from his research and accept appointment as dean of Yale College, because he thought the sciences should be more strongly represented in the university's academic leadership. He hoped that the appointment would lead to the strengthening of science in the curriculum, and it later did: under Altman's leadership a third course in the sciences was added to the requirements for graduation from Yale College, two of them to be in the physical sciences. Another of the appointments in the last years of Giamatti's presidency was of Leon Rosenberg, an academic geneticist, as dean of the School

of Medicine; Rosenberg initiated and led, with Giamatti's enthusiastic support, a capital drive for the school successfully
completed after Giamatti had left.

Financial constraints also dictated what Yale could do for
its graduate schools. Giamatti knew that they were important.
In his 1979 homily on the sciences, he affirmed that "the
strength of Yale College derives in large part from the presence
of the professional schools around it." Yale's modest financial
support of New Haven is less easily explained by budgetary
considerations; Giamatti was philosophically skeptical of the
duty—or the right—to apply educational resources to municipal purposes, even in Yale's home city. But during Giamatti's
tenure such issues were academic. Who knows what would
have been done had resources been greater?

The assertion that Giamatti neglected during his presidency the cause of curriculum reform is exaggerated. When he
took office, the process of reinstating mandatory requirements
abandoned in the 1960s was inching forward. By early 1978
undergraduates were required to complete at least two courses
in each of four categories: the humanities, the arts, the "administrative" (that is, social) sciences, and the natural sciences
(including computer science, engineering, and mathematics).
During the Giamatti years, the course of study was tightened
to require undergraduates to acquire basic competence in at
least one foreign language. Further changes made thereafter
during Altman's deanship added one additional required
course in each of the four categories, at least two of those in
science to be taken in the physical sciences.

Another decade passed before Yale, in the administration
of Richard Levin, blessed with the robust economy of the Clinton years, a popular long-serving dean of Yale College, Richard
Brodhead, and the occasion of the university's three hun-
dredth birthday, could undertake an expensive, and inevitably

controversial, comprehensive revision of its undergraduate curriculum. Curriculum reform is only one of the issues unfinished by his predecessors that the Levin administration has successfully addressed. Its remarkable achievements have had the unintended but inevitable negative consequence of emphasizing even more dramatically in the light of hindsight the travails and omissions of the Giamatti era.

Near the end of his long life (he was over ninety when he died in 2001), Yale's legendary humanist teacher and scholar Maynard Mack, so close to Giamatti as friend and mentor throughout the younger man's years at Yale, said to an admirer of Giamatti that the two important things about him were his extraordinary charisma and his vision of the nature and purpose of an ideal university as expressed in the homilies. Mack had nothing to say about Giamatti's stewardship of Yale as its president—either his accomplishments or his failures. He simply didn't think they were important—Giamatti did what he had to do. For Mack, Giamatti established the success of his presidency by expressing, with rare eloquence and for all to hear, timeless truths about the right role of education in a democratic society, whatever the academic fashions of the moment. This assessment stands in contrast to the verdict of Alvin Kernan, who is unable to separate what Giamatti said from the hard realities of the "new university," which, Kernan concludes, "destroyed his presidency." Kernan believes that the Giamatti story "is a tragic one," certainly not a success.

Success is, of course, very much in the eye of the beholder. Would it be more illuminating to evaluate Giamatti's presidency by a different criterion, its importance rather than its success? An observer with broad credentials in appraising educational leaders, himself unaffiliated with Yale, has suggested three separate criteria for measuring the importance of a university president: Did he encounter, and successfully address, during his presidency a set of problems reflecting some significant tendency or dilemma in universities in general or in the larger society? Or did he preside over changes in his own institution that represent a major contribution to the evolution of higher education? Or did he contribute an influential new thesis or innovation in higher education through his writings? Each of these three criteria readily brings to mind flesh-and-blood prototypes. Kingman Brewster's steady leadership during America's tumultuous sixties, which included presiding over the historic introduction of women and admission by academic merit into Yale College, qualifies him under the first of them. The second criterion describes Charles W. Eliot, who built Harvard's great graduate schools, and who left his own particular mark by creating the elective system allowing students choice in their own courses of study. Among college presidents whose writings remain influential are Robert Maynard Hutchins at the University of Chicago, advocate for a course of study based upon the "great books" of the Western canon to realize in the twentieth century Cardinal Newman's nineteenth-century vision of a liberal education; and, in our own time, Clark Kerr of the University of California, whose 1963 Godkin Lectures at Harvard, as supplemented from time to time, became *The Uses of the University,* the classic description of the modern research university and its special tensions and problems.

Is it possible to find a place for A. Bartlett Giamatti among these giants? It is hard to see where. Maynard Mack would have classified him among the influential writers, but that is not the consensus among professional educators. Notwithstanding his unique emphasis on the function of a liberal education to teach the art of civil discourse for the purpose of constructive citizenship, he is for most of them simply another voice extolling the wares of the university. If his presidency was important, it is for a different reason.

The values expressed in Giamatti's homilies have little of Kernan's "new university" in them. They are in fact—like all of his career—in large part a repudiation of it. Can a university president so out of touch with the prevailing ethos of his institution be considered "important"? Ironically, there is a case to be made for Giamatti's lasting significance in the very existence of the inhospitable environment that surrounded him, for it provided a background against which what he was and what he said stood out in dramatic profile. Thus for many he was a hero, defending and living out timeless values with eloquence and the humor of an irresistible charisma in a troubled and destructive time. Important? That value, too, like success, may lie in the eye of the beholder.

Baseball

The Green Fields of the Mind

Maynard Mack, in his remarks about Giamatti at the memorial service for him at Yale, observed that as a teacher "he transcended all others . . . in his ability to sustain at all times that multiple perspective which can hold [apparently unrelated ideas] in a single astonishing tableau." Nowhere do we see this more clearly than in his writings on sports, specifically baseball, where echoes of and parallels to his other concerns are constantly present. The multiple perspective is dramatically at work in a slim volume published shortly after his death entitled *Take Time for Paradise,* where at the outset sports are likened to the Garden of Eden, Giamatti's pervasive symbol for the coexistence of freedom and order.

Sports are like paradise, Giamatti says, because they offer what he calls "freedom untrammeled"—that is, outcomes without consequence, "where every choice is free from error." He recalls Milton's Garden of Eden in *Paradise Lost,* where the only stricture is not to touch the fruit of the tree of Knowledge of Good and Evil, and Adam says to Eve,

> let us not think hard
> One easy prohibition, who enjoy
> Free leave so large to all things else, and choice
> Unlimited of manifold delights.

"Save for the prohibition," Giamatti writes, "those lines capture the essence . . . of leisure better than any I know, the ideal to which our play aspires:

> Free leave so large to all things . . . and choice
> Unlimited of manifold delights."

The other attribute of paradise, inseparable from freedom, is order. Order is imposed in sports by rules, what Giamatti calls the "basic convention" for any game—the assumption of a level playing field, where the result is determined by merit. The cardinal sin against the rules is cheating, which strikes at the heart of this basic convention. We will need to remember, when we consider the Pete Rose affair, that for Giamatti Rose's conduct was an affront to the order that is the basic convention of the paradise of baseball.

The final chapter of Giamatti's little treatise on sports is entitled "Baseball as Narrative," and in it he lays out the particular characteristics of that sport—the unique combination of freedom and order—that make it a special paradise of its own. Giamatti is first of all fascinated by baseball's precise and unvarying dimensions, which he describes in loving detail:

> The field . . . consists of a square whose four sides are ninety feet long; this square is tipped so that a "diamond" is enchased in the grass. Not quite in the middle of the square, sixty feet, six inches from home plate, is a circle, with a radius of nine feet, at whose center (we are on the pitcher's mound) is a "rectangular slab of whitened rubber, 24 inches by six inches."
> . . . The circle of the mound faces a larger circle around home plate, whose radius is thirteen feet, . . . which contains the rectangles of the batter's boxes and the area for umpire and

catcher. At the center of this circle . . . is the source of the macro dimensions, the point of reference for all the medium and larger geometric shapes, the only shape on the field that does not figure the eternal and universal outlines and meanings of square and circle. We are at home plate, the center of all the universes, the *omphalos*, the navel of the world.

"Squares containing circles, containing rectangles," Giamatti writes; "precision in counterpoint with passion; order compressing energy." He continues: "The geometry of the field that extends the threes and fours gives us as well the deep patterns that order the narrative—three strikes, three bases, nine players, nine innings; four bases (including home) or four balls." All of this provides the order within which the freedom of the game may be expressed. "Organized by the metric of the game, by the prosody of the play, is all the random, unpredictable, explosive energy of playing, crisscrossing the precise shapes in lines and curves, bounces and wild hops and parabolas and slashing arcs." And it takes place in an enclosed green space that is itself a garden suggestive of paradise.

But if baseball with its blend of order and freedom is like a garden paradise, it is also for Giamatti, the Spenserian, like another of his preoccupations; it belongs, like *The Faerie Queene,* to the literary genre called epic romance. A characteristic theme of the genre is the need to return home after the quest—its prototypical expression is *The Odyssey* of Homer, the account of the long and dangerous return of the hero to Ithaca and Penelope after the Trojan War. The fourth base in baseball, Giamatti reminds us, is not called a base. It is home plate; and like home in the epic romance, it is both the starting place of the adventure and the goal to which the hero seeks to return. The journey begins at home, negotiates the twists and turns of the bases and all their dangers, and if the attempt to return home succeeds,

and it is given one to round third, a long journey seemingly
over, the end in sight, then the hunger for home, the drive to
rejoin one's earlier self and one's fellows, is a pressing, growing, screaming in the blood. . . .
　　If the attempt, long in planning and execution, works,
then the reunion and all it means is total—the runner is a
returned hero, and the teammates are for an instant all true
family.

Here is a striking example of Giamatti's imaginative impulse
and his capacity to see his enthusiasms in multiple perspective.
　　For Giamatti, baseball, an earthly replica of paradise, has
other significances. Though the game is not bound by time—it
is perhaps unique among team sports in that respect—it is
bound *in* time to the rhythm of the seasons. Here is an excerpt
from an essay entitled "The Green Fields of the Mind":

　　It breaks your heart. It is designed to break your heart. The
　　game begins in the spring, when everything else begins again,
　　and it blossoms in the summer, filling the afternoons and
　　evenings, and then as soon as the chill rains come, it stops and
　　leaves you to face the fall alone. You count on it, rely on it to
　　buffer the passage of time, to keep the memory of sunshine
　　and high clouds alive, and then just when the days are all
　　twilight, when you need it most, it stops. Today, October 2, a
　　Sunday of rain and broken branches and leaf-clogged drains
　　and slick streets, it stopped, and summer was gone. . . . Out
　　here, on Sunday, October 2, where it rains all day, Dame Mu-
　　tability never loses.

"I see great things in baseball. It's our game, the American
game," wrote Walt Whitman. Giamatti, too, sees the uniquely
American quality of the game as one of its significances. He
spoke of this quality in a talk he gave in 1985 to the Massachusetts Historical Society entitled "Baseball and the American Character." In it he emphasized, first, the metaphor we
have already seen: the pattern in baseball of leaving and re-

turning home. "For what is . . . so much of the American experience about," he asked, "but looking for home, . . . a nation of immigrants always migrating in search of home, . . . the American desire to start over in the great green garden, Eden or Canaan, of the New World."

Finally, baseball is America's game because the game and the country grew up together. Giamatti reminds us that it has its origins in games played in prerevolutionary times: old cat, towne-ball, round ball. It achieved its nearly definitive form even before the Civil War, not through its "invention" by Abner Doubleday in 1839 in a field outside Cooperstown, New York (a myth, as Giamatti rightly says), but in Alexander Cartwright's Knickerbocker Base Ball Club in 1846, which played its games on a lovely open tract of land surrounded by trees on the Hudson River in Hoboken, New Jersey, called the Elysian Field. "The Biblical imagery of wilderness and garden from Genesis, the Canticles, Revelation 12," Giamatti says, "is caught up in the image of Elysium. It is meet and right that this place is the birthplace of our game."

These wonderful writings on baseball embody, with all of Giamatti's rare eloquence and imagination, his understanding and love of the sport as the expression of his deepest values. But like all lovers of baseball, he was at heart a fan, in his case of the Boston Red Sox. So we may close this chapter by returning to that team and its fortunes after Giamatti first fell in love with it in South Hadley in the 1940s.

The 1950s and the first half of the 1960s were unprofitable ones for the Boston team. From 1951 through 1966 the Red Sox never finished closer than eleven games behind the American League champion. All of the suspense of a pennant race was gone by Memorial Day. In the last of those years it won seventy-two games and lost ninety, finishing in next-to-last place. But the following year the Red Sox reversed those numbers and, in a feverish four-team pennant race that went down to the last day of the season, became American League champions. In that remarkable season, remembered as the Impossible Dream by Red Sox Nation (for so their fans are collectively called), they were led by their new star, Carl Yastrzemski, whom Giamatti had the pleasure of inducting into baseball's Hall of Fame in his only year as Commissioner of Baseball.

The Red Sox lost the 1967 World Series in seven games (the maximum) to a much superior National League champion, the St. Louis Cardinals, but there was no shame in it. During the next few years they were an above-average team but did not win a championship. They came close in 1972, losing the divisional title only in the final series of the season, and they would have won in 1974 save for a horrendous late-season collapse. In 1975, however, they won again, this time losing the World Series to another superior National League champion, the Cincinnati Reds, in seven games. Many believe it was the finest World Series ever played: in six of the seven games, the winning team came from behind; in five games the winning margin was one run; there were two extra-inning games, and two games were settled in the ninth inning. Most memorable was Carlton Fisk's home run in the twelfth inning of game six to win it for the Red Sox after they had tied it in the eighth inning, also on a home run. Like the lost World Series of 1967, it seemed almost a triumph, though the drought of world championships visited on the Red Sox by the Curse of the Bambino was not broken.

But in 1978 the horror of heartbreaking loss recurred, this time when the weak-hitting New York Yankees infielder Bucky Dent won a one-game winner-take-all playoff at Fenway Park for the American League East championship, erasing a Red Sox lead and snatching away what seemed a sure victory with a windblown seventh-inning home run that nestled into the net just over the short left field wall in the corner nearest to home plate. The new Yale president Bart Giamatti saw this home run not at Fenway Park but on television at the airport in Austin, Texas, as he waited for a flight to New York. "There was, for me," he later wrote (in an essay entitled "Recall as the Series Ends, the Afternoon of the Fall"), "a sense that an even older law had asserted again its iron hand. . . . There was nothing more, no easy answers, and no turning back. . . . I am waiting for the journey to end, since I heard the final score, so that when spring comes we may start for home again."

This chapter began with Maynard Mack's observation of Giamatti's capacity to hold apparently unrelated ideas through multiple perspective "in a single astonishing tableau." Mack offered as an example the yoking together of Spenser and the Red Sox in the essay from which the account of Bucky Dent's home run comes:

> The Old Poet said, "Nothing is sure that grows on earthly ground." He had seen the tides of instinct in us all and the flux of matters mortal, and he knew the only constant is corrosive change.
>
> He made of that knowledge a goddess, Dame Mutability, and gave her sway over all things below the moon. He was a melancholy man and sang in a plangent, elegiac tone. He thought he knew it all.
>
> He did not. He had never loved the Red Sox.

National League President and Commissioner of Baseball

Giamatti's appointment as president of the National League did not take effect until the end of 1986, and before it did, an unexpected indignity befell him. In that year, his beloved Boston Red Sox won the American League pennant and entered the World Series in October against the New York Mets in search of their first world championship since 1918. They won the first two games in New York's Shea Stadium, won one of the next three in their home Fenway Park, and returned to New York needing to win only one of the final two games to take the Series. The sixth game went into extra innings. In the first half of the tenth the Red Sox scored two runs. When the first two Met batters went out in the last half of the inning, the Red Sox seemed to have won a World Series at last. The TV cameras were set up in the Red Sox clubhouse; the champagne was chilled. But it was not to be. The Mets scored three runs with two men out, the winning run coming on a ground ball that went between the legs of the Boston first baseman. The Mets again came from behind to win the seventh game.

For every Red Sox fan, game six of the 1986 World Series is

the ultimate expression of the Curse of the Bambino that Bart Giamatti had lived with since his boyhood days in South Hadley. He was, of course, there to witness it in person, sitting in a box seat near the field as president-designate of the National League and thus, officially, bound to support the New York Mets, whatever his personal loyalties. He has described how he felt: "Something deeper, older, more primeval took over. There were gurgling noises coming from within my body. I found myself telling [the Red Sox manager] how to manage from the wrong box and yelling remarks I don't remember." Giamatti's institutional duty to represent the National League could not lessen the pain. His friend Roger Angell, the nonpareil of baseball chroniclers, ran into the "miserably victorious" Giamatti after the game. He "looked worn and wan," Angell wrote, "like Odysseus thrown up on still another beach: a man wrung dry by the gods."

Giamatti entered into his new responsibilities at the league offices on Park Avenue in New York in late 1986. His wife and family remained behind in New Haven, so he lived in an apartment in the city from Monday to Thursday each week, returning home for the weekend. He had been on the job a mere two weeks when he was howling to Vincent that he was bored and had to get out. But as time went by he grew into it. He especially enjoyed working with the umpires. He liked many of them personally, and he respected what they did: they were the enforcers of the order that he cherished in all things and thought supremely exemplified in baseball. He cemented his relationship with them in his first year by intervening, with his American League counterpart Bobby Brown, in stalled negotiations for an extension of their collective bargaining agreement with baseball, and settling the dispute just before the opening of the 1987 season on terms close to what the umpires were asking. The offer that baseball reportedly had had on the table before Giamatti and Brown joined the negotiations was, Giamatti said, "outmoded." The umpires would now be paid at a level "nearly commensurate with the great contributions they make to the game."

Consistent with his respect for the rules that the umpires enforced, Giamatti soon established himself as a "law and order" president. Two episodes will illustrate. In the summer of 1987, Kevin Gross, a pitcher for the Philadelphia Phillies, was found to have sandpaper affixed to, and a sticky substance on, his glove. Such illegal aids make it possible to mar or deface a baseball so that its trajectory in flight can be altered. Gross was suspended for ten days. His suspension was appealed on the grounds that it was an unduly harsh penalty for violation of a rule that explicitly provides only that an offender is to be ejected from the game in which the violation occurs. The appeal was denied by Giamatti. There is nothing, he wrote, to prevent baseball from imposing a sanction that goes beyond what the rule requires.

In the opinion that accompanied his ruling, Giamatti contrasts impulsive acts of violence on the field that, however inexcusable, grow out of the competitive nature of the game, with cheating, "acts of a cool, deliberate, premeditated kind."

> They are secretive, covert acts that strike at and seek to undermine the basic foundation of any contest declaring the winner —that all participants play under identical rules and conditions. Acts of cheating destroy that necessary foundation and thus strike at the essence of a contest. They destroy faith in the games' integrity and fairness; if participants and spectators alike cannot assume integrity and fairness, and proceed from there, the contest cannot in essence exist.

Here is Giamatti applying in a concrete situation the sentiments on cheating that, as we saw in the last chapter, he expressed in *Take Time for Paradise*. He was pleased with his opinion. He told Roger Angell that he had "worked as hard on my response to the Kevin Gross appeal as I worked on anything I did while I was in New Haven."

A second episode demonstrating Giamatti's emphasis on law and order in the game occurred the following spring. The issue was not cheating but physical abuse of an umpire, baseball's authority figure. It was a cold Saturday night in April at Riverfront Stadium, home of the Cincinnati Reds, who were playing the New York Mets before a capacity crowd, many of them surely fortified by drink on a weekend night against the early spring chill. There had been a couple of controversial calls in the early innings of a close game, enough to create an incendiary atmosphere ready to explode. In the ninth inning, with the score tied, the Mets advanced a runner to second base with two out. The next batter hit a hard ground ball into the shortstop hole, nearly a hit into left field, but stylishly fielded by the shortstop, who made the long throw to first. It was going to be a close play. The throw beat the runner, but the umpire, Dave Pallone, called him safe, ruling that the throw had pulled the first baseman off the bag. As the first baseman turned to argue with Pallone, he forgot about the Mets runner, who, off with the pitch, came around to score what proved to be the winning run.

Pete Rose, the fiery manager of the Reds, whose monumental clash with organized baseball is the subject of the next chapter, stormed off the bench onto the field to argue the call. He and Pallone went nose to nose, each brandishing a menacing finger in the other's face, until the infuriated Rose gave the umpire a vigorous shove backward with his forearm. Pallone immediately ejected him from the game, and as he turned to walk away, Rose shoved him again, from behind. The crowd went berserk. Objects of all kinds were thrown on the field, most of them harmless, but some—whiskey bottles, for example—potentially deadly missiles. When a boom box landed near home plate, the umpires suspended play and left the field. It was fifteen minutes before play was resumed. Pallone remained in the clubhouse.

It was a terrifying outburst, the worst riot in baseball in many years. Giamatti rightly believed that Rose, an icon to Reds fans, was the responsible instigator. He suspended Rose for thirty days and fined him $10,000, the stiffest penalty imposed on a participant in forty years. When Rose's appeal of the sanction was unsuccessful, he accepted it without further ado. But it must have left him with the feeling, when he and Giamatti clashed again, over Rose's gambling, that Giamatti, then the commissioner, was not his friend.

Giamatti's rigorous enforcement of the rules against cheating and abuse of umpires reflected the respect for order that informed all that he did and said as an academic. But he also brought with him from the university a respect for continuity and tradition. We see it clearly in his concern for baseball's written legacy that continued throughout his brief career as a major league executive.

Shortly after he became president of the National League, he was, in accordance with prevailing custom, elected to the board of directors of the Baseball Hall of Fame, the game's shrine and museum in Cooperstown, New York. It did not take him long to learn that the museum library was a neglected stepchild—housed in a small separate building in the rear, underfunded, understaffed, underappreciated. When baseball's management people and key staff assembled in New York in early 1987 for their annual planning sessions, Giamatti asked the chairman of the board to bring around to his office the librarian, Tom Heitz, who was questioned at length about the library's problems and deficiencies. From this and subsequent meetings there was conceived a plan for a spacious addition to the museum to house a new library and archive. Conservation of existing materials would be insured, and an ambitious program would be instituted to gather—from the office of the commissioner of baseball, from all the teams in organized baseball, and from other sources—a vastly expanded written record of the history of the game for use by scholars and others.

Planning for the new addition proceeded throughout Giamatti's tenure as a baseball executive. The project was finally approved in August 1989, a month before his death. Money now had to be raised and planning begun for the library and archive the new space was to house, and Giamatti's successor as commissioner, Fay Vincent, was in every way supportive. Major league teams were asked to act as bellwethers in the fund-raising effort, and some of them generously did, among them the Boston Red Sox, now controlled by Giamatti's friend Jean Yawkey, widow of the team's longtime owner. But by the fall of 1992 Vincent was gone, and the library-archive project, never without its detractors on the Hall of Fame board, languished. By the time the addition was opened in 1994, plans to cannibalize the space for museum purposes were well under way. The space on the second floor that was to house the library became offices for curators of ever-growing exhibits, and while some storage space remains, the active part of the project is limited to a modest reading room on the first floor, over which the librarian and archivist preside. It is named the A. Bartlett Giamatti Research Center, a mere shell of what its namesake originally envisioned.

Giamatti once described to Roger Angell, in expansive detail, what he called "the daily and weekly procession of administrative detail that marches across [my] desk." Perhaps. But he conceded that much of it had to do with disputed plays, field incidents, and rules infractions—that is, order within the game and the role of umpires. He conceded also that a very large part of the other detail involved dealings with the press. This observation draws attention to an enormously important role played by Giamatti the baseball executive: as the premier publicist of the game to the outside world. Much of this contribution was in the form of newspaper and magazine articles about him. Newsmen were naturally attracted to this articulate and available man, often seen at games and always ready to talk. They were also fascinated by his (to them) unlikely transition from a career as a literary scholar to the world of baseball. A computer search of newspaper and magazine pieces about Giamatti produces an astonishing number of items, most of them repetitive and unenlightening, but all of them presumably read by some audience, large or small.

Giamatti's own writings on baseball, though mostly predating his career as a baseball executive, were another important part of his role as a publicist for the game. We have sampled some of them in the previous chapter. Most of the pieces examined there were originally speeches, or essays written for local publications. But in 1977 he was engaged by *Harper's* magazine, prestigious and with a national circulation, to produce two articles a year on some aspect of athletics. The arrangement lapsed when in the following year he became president of Yale. But his first article, "Tom Seaver's Farewell," was widely read and praised as an example of Giamatti's capacity to see in baseball a reflection of larger issues.

As every baseball fan knows, Tom Seaver pitched for the New York Mets for a decade beginning in 1967. He was during that period perhaps the best pitcher in baseball, so outstanding that after his career he was inducted into the Hall of Fame in his first year of eligibility. The Mets were a woeful last-place team when he joined them. Two years later, in 1969, he pitched them into the World Series. In 1977 the Mets traded him after a salary dispute. To Giamatti the trade was more than a controversial personnel decision. It was an affront to baseball itself, for, as he writes, while other great athletes "are only superb at playing their sports, Seaver seems to embody his."

We have seen from his other writings on baseball that Giamatti saw in the game the combination of freedom and order that he treasured in all institutions and in life. He found these qualities in Seaver the athlete, a fastball strikeout pitcher, "brilliantly blending control and speed, those twin capacities for restraint and release that are the indispensable possessions of the great artist." He found them also in Seaver the young man, whom he contrasts with the protestors and flower children of the same era, "the great wave against structure and restraint." "This was a pastoral time," he recalls, "and it would, like all pastorals, turn sere, but for three or four years, while Seaver was gaining control over a block of space approximately three feet high, eighteen inches wide, and sixty feet six inches long, many other of America's 'young' were breaking loose."

Finally, he praises Seaver for his "dignity that manifested itself in an air of utter self-possession without any self-regard," and for "his sense of self-worth and . . . his conviction that you work by the rules, and that you are rewarded, therefore, according to the rules of merit." The management of the Mets, he concludes, had failed to understand that "among all the men who play baseball there is, very occasionally, a man of such qualities of heart and mind and body that he transcends even the great and glorious game, and that such a man is to be cherished, not sold."

The most elaborate and widely circulated introduction of Giamatti as baseball's premier publicist to the outside world was written not by Giamatti himself but by his great friend and admirer Roger Angell, in a piece entitled "Celebration" that appeared in *The New Yorker* magazine in August 1988. The two

men had met years before when Giamatti was president of
Yale. Angell had come to New Haven in the spring of 1981 to
cover a tournament college game between Yale and St. John's
University. By prearrangement he was seated next to Smokey
Joe Wood, then ninety-one years old, who had been Yale's baseball coach from 1923 to 1942. Far more important, Wood had
been a celebrated right-handed fireball pitcher for the Boston
Red Sox in the early part of the century, best remembered for
the 1912 season, when he won thirty-four games and led the
Red Sox to the World Series and a world championship. During that season he had won, by a score of 1-0, a famous pitcher's
duel against Walter Johnson of the Washington Senators, the
most revered pitcher of his day and (with Babe Ruth, Ty Cobb,
Honus Wagner, and Christy Mathewson—legends all) one of
the five charter members of baseball's Hall of Fame. Angell and
Wood talked about that game as part of Wood's reminiscences
during the college game on the field.

Angell wrote about the afternoon later that summer in a
piece in *The New Yorker* entitled "The Web of the Game." The
college game itself had been memorable, a pitcher's duel between Ron Darling of Yale and Frank Viola of St. John's, both of
whom later had productive big league careers. Darling carried
a no-hitter into the twelfth inning, when St. John's finally got a
hit and scored the only run of the game. The game and the
reminiscences became for Angell an exercise in baseball's continuity, the seamless historical web of the game. His piece
concludes:

> Somebody will probably tell Ron Darling that Smokey Joe
> Wood was at the game that afternoon and saw him pitch
> eleven scoreless no-hit innings against St. John's, and some-
> day . . . it may occur to him that his heartbreaking 0-1 loss in
> May, 1981, and Walter Johnson's 0-1 loss at Fenway Park in
> September, 1912, are now woven into the fabric of baseball.

Pitch by pitch, inning by inning, Ron Darling had made that happen. He stitched us together.

Giamatti did not meet Roger Angell that afternoon, but he read his piece, and a few days later Angell received a handwritten note on the letterhead of Yale's Office of the President addressed to "Mr. Angell," thanking him for his "lovely, unsentimental and rich piece," and confessing (Giamatti the baseball traditionalist is speaking here) that the "last sentences brought out of me a gasp of admiration at the fitness of the conclusion and the completeness of the whole." Giamatti wrote that he did not "wish to annoy," but asked if he might introduce himself to Angell in New York. The two men became friends.

"Celebration" is Angell's account of an evening spent with Giamatti at a Mets game at Shea Stadium. Angell had invited Giamatti "not from any desire to ferret out his views on the late news or the smoldering issues of the game or to quiz him about the commissionership [Giamatti had not yet been appointed] (by unspoken agreement, we never discussed it at all) but from the prospect of listening to a lifetime .400 talker strut his stuff in the proper setting." And what happened that evening was the "celebration" to which the title of the piece refers. The men talked about the pervasive element of repetition in baseball: a flow of like attempts by a succession of batters to leave home and return to it. "Even talking about it, it's O.K. to repeat ourselves," Angell said. "Absolutely," Giamatti replied. "We participate in the epic by talking about it while it is in progress. It's a celebration."

And so we hear the "lifetime .400 talker" on a whole variety of subjects while the game (pitched by Yale's Ron Darling for the Mets) is in progress: on his agenda as league president; on literature and the Red Sox; on the reaction of the press to his transition from academia to baseball ("when Pat Moynihan [a former Harvard professor] was campaigning for the Senate for the first time, his opponent early in some television debate called him 'Professor.' Pat threw up his hands and said, 'Uh-oh —the mudslinging starts!' "); about modern ballparks ("the most conventional architecture since Mussolini's social realism"); on fans who come to games to see their friends, to drink, to listen to the rock music and watch the ads and quizzes on the electronic scoreboard (for them "baseball isn't interesting or entertaining enough on its own. They're like theatrical companies who only want to do Shakespeare in motorcycle boots and leather jackets. They've given up on the beautiful language").

In "Celebration" Roger Angell gave to a broad readership an introduction to baseball's premier publicist in all his verbal glory.

Soon afterward Peter Ueberroth announced that he would resign as commissioner of baseball effective April 1, 1989, and Giamatti was unanimously chosen by the owners to succeed him. When the offer to become commissioner came, Giamatti asked Fay Vincent to represent him in contract negotiations. The contract that Vincent drafted was heavily tilted in his client's favor, providing not only for a substantial salary but for unusually generous continuing payments if Giamatti should die during the contract's five-year term. Vincent warned his client that the proposed terms would be considered outrageous by the owners and would probably need to be modified, but baseball accepted them without objection, and when Giamatti died, having served as commissioner for only five months, the financial security he had sought for his family was realized. A favorable contract was not Vincent's only favor to the new commissioner. His days at Coca-Cola were coming to an end, and he agreed to serve Giamatti as deputy commissioner, bringing his wide experience as an executive to the partnership. "I could think of nothing nicer than to get up in the morning and work for baseball and be with Bart," he later told an interviewer. "To me that was very close to nirvana." The commissioner of baseball is in charge of a big business. His office, with a large staff, is among other things concerned with licensing baseball properties—logos, souvenirs, clothing, equipment, and the like; negotiating national television and radio contracts; resolving disputes between owners; and supervising regular-season scheduling and arrangements for the All-Star Game and the World Series. The commissioner himself is of course ultimately responsible for the proper performance of these duties, and Giamatti could not escape them. But he had in Fay Vincent as his deputy a seasoned businessman to whom he could delegate much of the daily supervisory burden. This was increasingly necessary as Giamatti became embroiled in a titanic battle of wills with Pete Rose over allegations that Rose had bet on baseball games in violation of the game's most basic prohibition.

The Pete Rose Affair

G ambling has long been the scourge of baseball. In the earliest days, when the game was played as genteel recreation by members of upper-class social clubs like the New York Knickerbockers, modest wagering among participants and observers seemed no more than a harmless amusement. But after the Civil War, as baseball became a professional sport with salaried players, serious gamblers were attracted to it. It was commonplace for them to be in the stands, taking bets and trying to influence outcomes. Later in the nineteenth century, as baseball grew into the national pastime, its leaders tried hard to achieve respectability for the game, and gambling was largely brought under control. But when the government shut down the nation's racetracks during the First World War, the professional gamblers returned, and there were constant rumors that games were being fixed. The ultimate result was the fixing of the 1919 World Series, when a group of players on the plainly superior Chicago White Sox (ever thereafter known as the Black Sox) took bribes to throw the Series to the Cincinnati Reds.

Baseball's response to this crisis was the establishment of

the position of commissioner, and the appointment as the first commissioner of an autocratic and moralistic federal judge named Kenesaw Mountain Landis. Landis insisted on virtually unlimited power over every club and every participant, all of whom were required to submit to the commissioner's discipline and to waive their rights of access to the courts to review his actions. He asserted his powers promptly. The offending players were tried in a Chicago courtroom under an indictment charging them with conspiracy to defraud the public. Though there seems to have been little doubt about the bribery and its result, they were all acquitted when the judge instructed the jury that the state must prove that the ballplayers intended to defraud the public, "and not merely to throw ballgames." Landis was unmoved. In a statement issued shortly after the verdict, he announced that "regardless of the verdict of juries, no player that throws a ball game, no player that entertains proposals or promises to throw a game, no player that sits in a conference with a bunch of crooked players and gamblers where the ways and means of throwing games are discussed, and does not promptly tell his club about it, will ever again play professional baseball." All of the offending players were banished for life, including one, the great third baseman Buck Weaver, who had known of the fix but had refused to participate in it.

Landis, of course, could hardly be content with punishing players who had already been corrupted by the gamblers. He wanted gambling out of baseball entirely, and he set about to fashion rules that would precisely notify participants in the game where the line was drawn. The result was what is now Major League Rule 21(d), which provides as follows:

> Any player, umpire, or club or league official or employee, who shall bet any sum whatsoever upon any baseball game in

connection with which the bettor has no duty to perform, shall be declared ineligible for one year.

Any player, umpire, or club or league official or employee, who shall bet any sum whatsoever upon any baseball game in connection with which the bettor has a duty to perform, shall be declared permanently ineligible.

To paraphrase: Bet on any baseball game and you're out for a year. Bet on your own team—to win or to lose—and you're out for life. Rule 21(d) is prominently posted in every baseball clubhouse and incorporated into every player's contract.

Early in 1989 the commissioner's office received information indicating that Pete Rose, the manager of the Cincinnati Reds, one of baseball's greatest players over a career of more than two decades, had violated both sections of Rule 21(d).

Rose had grown up in a working-class neighborhood of Cincinnati, the son of a bank accountant, who compensated for the frustrations of his dull job by participating in amateur sports. Pete was a small boy with limited athletic skills, but, encouraged by his father, he developed a passion for baseball. He played in a local sandlot league, then in American Legion ball, where his drive and desire enabled him to perform beyond the limitations of his natural talent. Fortunately for Pete, his uncle was a scout for the Cincinnati Reds, and when he graduated from high school, on the advice of his uncle the Reds signed him for a modest bonus and sent him to their lowest minor league farm team.

Rose was a scrappy second baseman who had taught himself through constant practice to be a switch-hitter—that is, to bat left-handed against right-handed pitchers and vice versa. The initial scouting reports on the young ballplayer were not promising. "Pete Rose can't make a double play, can't throw, can't hit left-handed and can't run," the first one read. But over the following winter he grew taller, heavier, and stronger, and the next summer, in Class D ball, he became an adequate fielder and a .300 hitter. He repeated his success the following year at the Class A level. By 1963, at the age of twenty-two, he was invited to spring training with the major league team and unexpectedly won the job as starting second baseman for the Cincinnati Reds. It was the beginning of a twenty-four-year major league career during which Pete Rose was a star, a lifetime .300 hitter, and the holder of two impressive records: for the most consecutive games with a base hit in National League history (forty-four, tied with the old-time player Willie Keeler), and, above all, for the most career hits in baseball history, 4,256, eclipsing Ty Cobb's fifty-year-old record of 4,191 hits that many people thought would never be broken. Rose seemed a sure bet for baseball's Hall of Fame when his career was over.

He was throughout his career a cocky, reckless overachiever. "Charlie Hustle," they called him, running full throttle to first base after a walk, sliding headlong into second or third stretching a single into a double or a double into a triple. On occasion his enthusiasm became manic. In the 1970 All-Star Game, racing to score the winning run in extra innings from second base on a teammate's single, he launched himself at the opposing catcher, Cleveland's Ray Fosse, like a human missile to avoid being tagged at home plate and inflicted a serious injury that effectively cut short Fosse's promising career. In a game against the New York Mets in the 1973 National League Championship Series, he bowled over the Mets shortstop Bud Harrelson with a similar dive, trying to break up a double play even though the ball had already been relayed to first base, then elbowed Harrelson in the face as they both got up, thus precipitating one of the worst player riots in modern baseball history. His compulsive behavior on the field was mirrored in his conduct out of uniform. His womanizing was egregious even among ballplayers, for whom the ready availability of so-called baseball Annies on the road made philandering a common thing. He shamelessly flaunted his mistresses in public in the presence of his teammates and fans. And he became a pathological gambler, a high roller at the racetrack and other sporting events, a compulsion that intensified as his playing career came to an end and he sought to compensate off the field for the lost excitement of playing. By the 1980s he was betting thousands of dollars nearly every day, at times falling hundreds of thousands of dollars in debt to his bookies.

The Major League Agreement governing the powers of the commissioner provides that he may "investigate . . . any act, transaction or practice charged, alleged or suspected to be not in the best interests of . . . baseball, . . . to determine, after investigation, what punitive action is appropriate . . . and to take such action." Giamatti's term of office as commissioner was not due to begin until April 1, but the outgoing commissioner, Peter Ueberroth, turned the Rose matter over to Giamatti and his deputy, Fay Vincent, and on their recommendation he appointed a Washington lawyer, John M. Dowd, a former Justice Department prosecutor, to conduct an investigation into the charges against Rose. On May 9 Dowd filed his report, which concluded that "the accumulated testimony of witnesses, together with the documentary evidence and telephone records reveal extensive betting activity by Pete Rose in connection with professional baseball and, in particular, Cincinnati Reds games, during the 1985, 1986, and 1987 baseball seasons." This conclusion was supported by 225 typed pages (and seven bound volumes of exhibits) of vivid and devastating detail. The report would be evidence at a hearing before the commissioner guaranteed to Rose by the Major League Agreement.

Rose's lawyers, of course, knew that Dowd had been conducting an investigation for the commissioner into Rose's alleged gambling activities, and, fully aware of Rose's gambling proclivities, they can hardly have been surprised at Dowd's conclusions. But it is no disparagement of their conduct to observe that they reacted as any good lawyer would who has a weak case: they kicked up a lot of dust and cried foul. The report is "appalling," wrote Robert A. Pitcairn, Jr., of the law firm representing Rose, in a letter to Dowd. It is "no more than the bellicose repetitive arguments of a prosecutor who knows he cannot make his case. . . . If this Report is your idea of fair play and natural justice, I feel sorry for you."

Some of the dust that was kicked up seems to have gotten into the eyes of James Reston, Jr., who in his generally excellent book on the Rose affair entitled *Collision at Home Plate* is highly critical of the conduct of both Dowd and Giamatti during the investigation of Rose's gambling. In order to assess the fairness of Reston's criticism, it is necessary to understand the limitations under which Dowd operated in conducting his investigation, and the means he employed to overcome them.

The commissioner of baseball has no power to subpoena witnesses or compel testimony. But the Major League Agreement does confer on him the authority to punish any player or other employee of baseball for conduct which, in his judgment, is "not in the best interests of baseball," and the courts have allowed him broad leeway in deciding what that phrase means. The rules of procedure for the conduct of proceedings by the commissioner's office require baseball personnel to produce documents and give evidence before him when summoned to do so, and failure to discharge this duty may be treated by him as not in the best interests of baseball and therefore grounds for the imposition of penalties, including suspension. In short, a player must cooperate in the investigation of his own conduct, and on the advice of his counsel Rose did so.

There is no doubt that Dowd made aggressive use of this advantage. He subjected Rose to an exhaustive deposition under oath, scheduled late enough in the investigation to allow Dowd to draw conclusions as to Rose's truthfulness on the basis of what he had already learned from others. Most important, he required Rose to submit handwriting samples under the supervision of a handwriting expert for use in determining whether betting slips made available by Rose's principal accuser, which showed bets on games of the Cincinnati Reds, were written by Rose.

Reston is particularly offended by the handwriting test to which Rose was subjected. He calls it "outrageous," conducted in an "essentially unfair strike force atmosphere," an egregious example of Dowd's "highly questionable investigation methods" that "ran roughshod over the normal constitutional protections that any ordinary criminal defendant would have had." But as Reston acknowledges, this was not a criminal proceeding but a private investigation conducted under ground rules, to which Rose had consented by signing a major league contract, that strongly encouraged his voluntary cooperation. Dowd was doing no more than any conscientious investigator would have been expected to do in taking advantage of those ground rules.

Dowd had no such leverage over sources not subject to the rules of baseball. He was nonetheless successful in obtaining evidence from two separate informants, each of whom had his own reason for cooperating. The first of these was one Paul Janszen, a low-level associate of petty crooks, who had met Rose in 1986 and by the following year had become his all-purpose flunky. His duties included placing bets for him. Rose was constantly delinquent in paying his bookies for lost bets, and on a few occasions Janszen ponied up the money out of his own pocket, expecting to be reimbursed by Rose in due course. But Rose was as careless about what he owed Janszen as he was of his debts to bookies, and when Janszen, who was hardly a wealthy man, had experienced the runaround on some forty thousand dollars he was owed by Rose, he turned vengeful, cooperating first with the FBI in an investigation of Rose's alleged tax evasion, and then with the Dowd investigation into Rose's gambling activities.

Janszen told Dowd's investigators in particular about Rose's betting on baseball during the five-week period between April 7 and May 13, 1987, when, he said, he had placed bets for Rose of two thousand dollars each on seven games every night, including games of the Cincinnati Reds. He provided his own written betting records to back up his testimony and, most important, he provided copies of three of Rose's own betting sheets, also showing bets on the Cincinnati Reds, that he had filched from Rose's home and turned over to the FBI to support what he had told them about Rose's gambling and thus establish his general credibility. Dowd's handwriting expert concluded that these sheets were indeed written by Rose, and though Dowd did not know it, the originals of two of the sheets in the possession of the FBI bore Rose's fingerprints. As Reston concedes, "between the handwriting and fingerprint evidence, the fact that Rose had bet on baseball on at least two occasions is absolutely and incontrovertibly established." This documentary evidence surely lent credence to the rest of Janszen's story, which was in any event extensively corroborated by telephone records and other sources.

But Reston expresses skepticism. He makes much of the fact that Janszen failed the first of two lie detector tests to which he was subjected. The Dowd report makes no secret of this fact. Believing that the first test was in some respects flawed, Dowd asked Janszen to take a second test, in which the questions related to specific instances of Rose's betting. Janszen passed this test. Reston's skepticism is surprising in light of the fact that in his extended summary of Rose's conduct, what Janszen told Dowd is largely stated as fact.

The second of Dowd's principal informants was a Cincinnati-based bookie named Ron Peters, who told Dowd's investigators (described by Reston as "baseball cops" and "strong-arm baseball men") that he had taken bets from Rose over a period from 1984 to 1987 in amounts of two thousand to five thousand dollars each, coming to about a million dollars in the aggregate, on games of professional football, basketball, and baseball. Peters's motivation for cooperating with Dowd was not revenge but self-interest, for Peters was awaiting sentencing for two counts of tax evasion and cocaine trafficking to which he had pleaded guilty, and Dowd had promised a commendatory letter from the commissioner to the sentencing judge in exchange for his cooperation.

Reston calls this arrangement a "devil's compact" and says that Dowd's recommendation to Giamatti that he furnish such a letter was "horrendously bad legal advice." These characterizations are not justified. Favorable communications to sentencing authorities are commonly used tools of prosecutors or investigators to obtain helpful testimony. The problem with the arrangement was not fundamental impropriety but the wording of the letter that Dowd prepared for Giamatti's signature, and the fact that the sentencing judge was the wrong jurist to send it to.

Giamatti had had no firsthand experience of Peters's testimony to Dowd's investigators. Nonetheless Dowd had him say in his letter, "I am satisfied that Mr. Peters has been candid, forthright and truthful with my special counsel." The letter was written before Giamatti had received Dowd's report, and certainly before he had conducted a hearing at which Rose would have an opportunity to contradict Peters's testimony. If he pronounced it "truthful" at this early stage, did it not mean that he had already decided Rose was guilty of betting on baseball, even before he had discharged his duty to be an impartial judge of the facts? It would surely have been better to put those words in the mouth of the investigator than to attribute them to the commissioner himself. Reston is critical of Giamatti for signing such a letter. "A man of Giamatti's sophistication and intellect should have known better," he writes. Intellect, certainly. But hardly the degree of sophistication that would lead a man who was not a lawyer to second-guess the draft of an adviser who was.

The letter was duly typed on the commissioner's letterhead and sent to the sentencing judge, Carl Rubin of Cincinnati, the senior judge of the federal district court for the Southern District of Ohio. As Reston says, "With a hundred different judges in different places in America, Giamatti's letter might have been just another unpersuasive letter in the file," but not with Judge Rubin. Reston describes him as "a bantam fighter: feisty, independent, strong-willed, with a hot temper that quickly flares." He was also an ardent fan of the Cincinnati Reds and a great admirer of Pete Rose, wholly out of sympathy with the investigation into Rose's gambling that the whole world knew Giamatti's office was conducting.

Judge Rubin hit the ceiling. More than that, Reston reports, he sent a copy of the letter to Rose's lead counsel, his old friend Reuven Katz, surely a highly irregular step for a federal judge. Katz saw immediately that the letter provided a basis for challenging Giamatti's impartiality. This perception became the basis for the legal strategy that Rose's lawyers now pursued.

Dowd's report was submitted to Rose's counsel on May 11, and a hearing was set for May 25. In the interim, Rose's lawyers communicated to Giamatti their demands: the "highly prejudicial" Dowd report should not be admitted into evidence at the hearing; the hearing should be governed by the established rules of evidence applicable in court proceedings; Rose's coun-

sel should be afforded adequate time to take depositions from
the witnesses Dowd had interviewed and to cross-examine
them; and finally, Giamatti should disqualify himself from further participation in the matter in any way. Giamatti's reply
came soon after: the Dowd report would be before him at the
hearing; he would not disqualify himself; he would postpone
the hearing for a month to allow Rose's counsel time to prepare
their case.

Rose's counsel now had to consider their options. They
could hardly be optimistic about the outcome of a hearing. On
the other hand, the prospects for success in litigation were
dim. The rules governing proceedings before the commissioner provided that they "shall be conducted in general like
judicial proceedings and with due regard for all the principles
of natural justice and fair play, but the Commissioner may
proceed informally whenever he deems it desirable." The commissioner should "in general follow the established rules of
evidence but may depart from them in cases in which the ends
of justice will in his judgment best be subserved by so doing."
The phrase "in general" in these formulations, Rose's lawyers
knew, took most of the legal force out of them. They also knew
that "natural justice and fair play" are laymen's words, without
the legal force of, say, "due process," whose precise meaning is
established by years of judicial precedent. They are what lawyers call "hortatory" standards, advisory and aspirational only.
And Rose would contend with a long history of legal decisions
establishing the near-dictatorial power of the commissioner.
The agreements and rules establishing the office of the commissioner, a judge had said in 1931, in language that had been
repeated with approval by courts as recently as the 1970s, "dis-
close a clear intent on the part of all parties to endow the
commissioner with all the attributes of a benevolent but abso-

lute despot and all the disciplinary powers of the proverbial pater familias."

But in the end, litigation was judged the lesser evil. Dowd's report would otherwise almost certainly be admitted into evidence. And the establishment of Giamatti's bias, though under court decisions grounds for his disqualification if proved, was a long shot solely on the strength of a letter he did not draft and scarcely read before signing. But the courts might provide for Rose that dear friend of a cause in trouble: delay. And from delay might come an acceptable result.

So a week before the rescheduled hearing by the commissioner, Rose filed suit against Giamatti in a state court in Ohio. The complaint is thirty-five typed pages long, alleging many things and asking for a variety of remedies, but the heart of it is the statement on the very first page that Pete Rose needed the intervention of the court "to protect and preserve his right to be judged in a fair hearing by an unbiased decisionmaker." Accordingly, the court was asked to rule that "it will be impossible for Pete Rose to have a fair hearing before Giamatti . . . on June 26, 1989 [the date of the rescheduled hearing] or any other time"; and since the Major League Agreement does not provide for a person other than the commissioner to conduct disciplinary proceedings when the commissioner must be disqualified because of bias, that the court itself determine whether or not Pete Rose bet on baseball. If this audacious request were to be granted, Rose's lawyers would have succeeded in moving the proceedings into a courtroom, where judicial rules of evidence apply that are not binding on the commissioner, and there would be a strong basis for excluding the Dowd report.

As a first step, Rose's lawyers asked the court to enter a temporary restraining order preventing Giamatti from proceeding with the scheduled hearing pending a final determination of the merits of the lawsuit, and this request was readily granted on the basis of a local judge's preliminary finding that Giamatti had prejudged the issue of Rose's gambling on baseball. It was the first move in a procedural chess game that was to occupy most of the rest of the summer of 1989. The commissioner's motion to suspend the temporary restraining order pending appeal was denied by the appellate court, and the order remained in effect. Rose's motion to dismiss the appeal was also denied. Giamatti's lawyers now succeeded in transferring the case from the state court of Ohio to a federal district court in that state under a statute that permits such a transfer where the parties to the controversy (in this case Rose and Giamatti) are citizens of different states. The applicability of that statute now itself became the subject of an appeal to a federal appellate court. Meanwhile, the federal district court judge who had approved the transfer left in effect the state court's original temporary restraining order preventing Giamatti from holding a hearing.

Thus matters stood in the second week in August. It was plain that the legal wrangling could go on indefinitely, and talks between the lawyers turned to possible settlement. Both sides had an incentive for settling. Fay Vincent, now taking a leading role in the resolution of the Rose matter, must have told Rose's lawyers that even if they succeeded in avoiding a finding of betting on baseball in violation of Rule 21(d), his admitted gambling on other sports and his habitual contact with lowlifes and undesirables provided ample grounds to banish him from baseball under the more general Rule 21(f) for conduct not in the best interests of baseball. So Rose was not going to win however the pending litigation came out. And if Rose's lawyers could negotiate his suspension without an admission that he had gambled on the Cincinnati Reds, there would be no such finding on the record when Rose exercised the right guaranteed him under the rules of baseball to apply for reinstatement after one year. If such an application were granted, Rose would have achieved all that really mattered to him: eligibility for election to the Baseball Hall of Fame.

For organized baseball the incentives to settle were different. Giamatti and Vincent felt that a prompt resolution of the Rose affair was essential for the image of the commissioner's office and of the game itself. It would not do for the public to conclude that baseball could not resolve its problems expeditiously. In this respect the delay that Rose's lawyers counted on when they decided to litigate paid dividends. Moreover, it was not good for baseball to have the commissioner publicly accused of being prejudiced and unfair, especially in a courtroom under the bright glare of media publicity. Nor, Vincent must have perceived, was it good for Giamatti himself. We saw during the labor crisis at Yale that he was particularly sensitive to attacks on his motives. He honestly believed that an investigation by independent counsel was the fairest way to deal with Rose, and while no one who had read Dowd's report could avoid being skeptical of Rose's innocence, Giamatti sincerely thought he could give proper weight to evidence to the contrary, if there was any. The suggestion of prejudice, particularly the constant attacks in the press on his presumed unfairness, wounded him. His distress was intensified by the inevitable delays of the legal process, intolerable for a chronically impatient man. "I had never seen Bart in so ugly a mood," Fay Vincent has written. "In that whole period, he was chain-smoking, barely sleeping, eating constantly, getting no exercise, getting pounded in the papers every morning and by the legal system the rest of the day." He was suffering, and his dear friend wanted the pain to stop.

So in the end a settlement was reached. Rose would consent to lifetime banishment from baseball but would not admit that he had gambled on baseball games. Under the rules of baseball, he would have the right to apply for reinstatement after a year. And while he was given no assurances whether or when such an application might be favorably acted upon, his lawyers were told by Giamatti that it would be received by him with an open mind if Rose had in the meantime mended his ways. As it turned out, Rose's stubborn and continued insistence that he did not have a gambling problem and thus did not need counseling, and the 1990 plea bargain that sent him to federal prison for evading taxes on income from his sales of signed baseball cards and memorabilia, rendered the right to apply for reinstatement academic. But his lawyers rightly felt at the time that they had achieved for him a highly favorable settlement in light of the facts.

On August 23, 1989, the settlement was announced at a press conference in New York. Giamatti read the statement that fixed him in the minds of Americans as the principled idealist he was. He defended the process by which the accusations against Rose were handled. "I believed then and believe now," he said, "that such a process, whereby an experienced professional inquires on behalf of the Commissioner as the Commissioner's agent, is fair and appropriate." He would follow it again "should any other occasion arise where charges are made or acts are said to be committed that are contrary to the interests of the game or that undermine the integrity of baseball."

Giamatti's statement continued with a ringing defense of baseball and its importance in American life that has become part of the game's legendary history:

> I say this so that there may be no doubt where I stand or why I stand there. I believe baseball is a beautiful and exciting game,

loved by millions—I among them—and I believe baseball is an important enduring American institution. It must assert and aspire to the highest principles—of integrity, of professionalism of performance, of fair play within its rules. . . . I will be told that I am an idealist. I hope so. I will continue to locate ideals I hold for myself and for my country in the national game as well as in other national institutions. And while there will be debate and dissent about this or that or another occurrence on or off the field, and while the game's nobler parts will always be enmeshed in the human frailties of those who, whatever their role, have stewardship of this game, let there be no doubt or dissent about our goals for baseball or our dedication to it. Nor about our vigilance and vigor—and patience—in protecting the game from blemish or stain or disgrace.

Coda

On the Friday of the week after Rose's banishment, September 1, 1989, Giamatti was dropped off on Martha's Vineyard by Fay Vincent, on his way in a chartered plane to his summer home on Cape Cod. Before Giamatti reached his Vineyard house in Edgartown, he was complaining of chest pains. An hour later he was dead of a massive heart attack. He was fifty-one years old. The news came to his shocked friends and admirers later in the day. Many of them can remember exactly where they were when they heard it, just as people remember where and how they learned of the death of Franklin Roosevelt or of John Kennedy. He was buried, after a graveside service attended by a few old friends, in the Grove Street Cemetery in New Haven, resting place of Yale presidents and other luminaries.

There were, of course, memorial services. Baseball held its tribute at Carnegie Hall in New York. Many baseball legends were present, including Giamatti's boyhood hero, Bobby Doerr, the Red Sox Hall of Fame second baseman of the 1940s; and Joe DiMaggio, who flew in from Japan to be there. Roger Angell was among the speakers. He wrote to Giamatti's widow later that "becoming a friend of his was an unexpected gift from the gods."

Yale's memorial service was held in Woolsey Hall, its large ceremonial auditorium, among those who had known him longest and who knew him best. Public eulogies and tributes are not necessarily the most reliable source of insight into the qualities of the person praised, but there is much to be learned about Giamatti's legacy to his friends and colleagues from the remarks made that afternoon. Benno Schmidt, his successor as Yale's president, speaking first, observed that "he did not so much lead as inspire." The nature of his capacity to inspire emerges from the remarks of others. Maynard Mack spoke of his "deeply held and deeply humane vision of the life of this community, this country, this world as it should be, obviously never would be, but must relentlessly be pursued as if it might be." Leon Rosenberg, his dean of the School of Medicine, referred to the rabbinical aphorism that, as we have seen, Giamatti included in his 1984 homily "Give Time to Time": "You are not required to complete the work, but neither are you free to desist from it." His close friend and colleague William Brainard, provost during most of his presidency, recalled lines from William Blake that Giamatti used to recite and that "will always remind me of Bart":

> Bring me my bow of burning gold!
> Bring me my arrows of desire!
> Bring me my spear! O Clouds, unfold!
> Bring me my chariot of fire!
>
> I will not cease from mental fight,
> Nor shall my sword sleep in my hand,
> Till we have built Jerusalem
> In England's green and pleasant land.

But what Giamatti inspired most in those whose lives were touched by him was affection. Lloyd Richards, whom Giamatti brought to Yale to succeed Robert Brustein as dean of the Yale

School of Drama, surely spoke for many when he concluded
his remarks with the words "I did not know A. Bartlett Giamatti
intimately. I loved him well." The observations of many people
after his death illustrate the point.

Linda Lorimer, now vice president and secretary of Yale,
was a junior member of the administration during the early
years of Giamatti's presidency. Recognizing her talent, he
plucked her from the general counsel's office in 1983 and made
her an associate provost. By 1984 she was an associate vice
president for human resources and a key member of Yale's
management team during the strike that year. She has written
about him as a boss. "He kidded us and he cared. Whether
writing a letter of welcome to my week-old daughter or taking
the time in the midst of an Ivy League President's meeting to
telephone with the reactions to a report I had helped prepare,
he himself worked to create the sense of community he championed." Her affection for him and his memory is palpable to
anyone today who talks to her about him.

Ella Scantlebury was in charge of the kitchen at Scroll and
Key, Giamatti's senior society, for many years. She was a leader
of New Haven's black community, active in city politics and for
a time city treasurer. Giamatti, always interested in anything
that had to do with New Haven, came to know her during his
year in the society. "He would come into the kitchen and chat
with me about politics in the city and how things were going,"
she recalled. "We got very close. When he was named president of the University, I was his honored guest at the table
when he was installed into office. He was like a son to me."

Giamatti and Fay Vincent first met when both men were
forty. Vincent has written at length about their friendship in his
recent book entitled *The Last Commissioner*. "It is rare," Vincent writes, "for a man after forty to make new and close
friends. . . . There is no need. But I was blessed: At forty, I made

a great and new friend, a friend who enriched me, changed me, challenged me, fascinated me." The friendship deepened over the years. Its depth is reflected in the impact on Vincent of Giamatti's death: "I had lost the brother I never had. . . . The loss was immense, totally unanticipated, even if it should have been. For a long while, I couldn't talk about Bart without choking up. I still miss him."

There were tangible expressions of affection for Giamatti, too. Scroll and Key contributed generously to the endowment at Yale of a graduate fellowship in his name. One tangible contribution came from an unexpected source. Giamatti was, Vincent has written, "the patron saint of umpires," and the umpires' union offered to pay for a tombstone marking his grave, an offer his widow accepted. The money came, unsentimentally but certainly appropriately, from the proceeds of a lawsuit filed by the union against a major league manager for slandering an umpire as corrupt after an unwelcome decision on the field. And there is, finally, that unadorned black granite bench in a corner of the Old Campus at Yale, commissioned and paid for by Giamatti's college classmates, with the inscription that summarizes his career: "A liberal education is at the heart of a civil society, and at the heart of a liberal education is the act of teaching." For as one of his colleagues said at the memorial service, "he never ceased to be a teacher."

Notes and Sources

General

The principal source for events at Yale, where Giamatti received all of his higher education and spent most of his adult years, was the *Yale Daily News,* available on microfilm in Yale's Sterling Memorial Library. Other sources, also available in the Yale Library, were the *Yale Weekly Bulletin and Calendar* and the *Yale Alumni Magazine.*

The Manuscripts and Archives section of the Yale Library contains files on Yale personnel and events. Of particular value were copies of Giamatti's speeches and other writings as president on various occasions and to various audiences ("Speeches and articles by and about Yale University presidents [RU 65], Manuscripts and Archives, Yale University Library").

Collision at Home Plate: The Lives of Pete Rose and Bart Giamatti, by James Reston, Jr. (New York: HarperCollins, 1991), contains the only extensive published biographical summary of Giamatti's life, and while particularly detailed in its account of the Pete Rose affair, has been a valuable source throughout for many other facts and observations. Also of value was Anthony Valerio's *Bart: A Life of A. Bartlett Giamatti by Him and About Him* (New York: Harcourt Brace Jovanovich, 1991).

Other important sources are noted below for the particular chapters to which they relate.

Boyhood

The principal sources for this chapter were personal interviews with Giamatti's mother, Peggy, his sister, Elria Ewing, and his brother, Dino. Also of value were personal interviews with Giamatti's boyhood friends William Mazeine and Andy Vitali.

A file on Valentine Giamatti in the Mount Holyoke Library Archives provided extensive information on his life and teaching career.

Valentine Giamatti's doctoral thesis is on file in the Harvard University Depository, available through Widener Library. His scholarly works referred to in the text are *Minimum of Italian Grammar* (New York: S.F. Vanni, 1947) and *Panoramic Views of the Inferno, Purgatory, and Paradise of Dante* (rpt. Holyoke, Mass.: Offset Printing Company, 1958).

Dan Shaughnessy's book is *The Curse of the Bambino* (New York: Dutton [Penguin USA], 1990).

Giamatti's eulogy of his father was delivered on April 15, 1982, at a memorial service in the Abbey Memorial Chapel at Mount Holyoke College. It is reprinted in the *Mount Holyoke Alumnae Quarterly*, Summer 1982, pp. 37–38.

Andover

Youth from Every Quarter: A Bicentennial History of Phillips Academy, Andover, by Frederick G. Allis, Jr. (Andover, Mass.: Phillips Academy, 1979), covers the 1950s. The quotation from the principal designer of the campus appears at pp. 372–73 of that volume.

Ruth Quattlebaum, the Andover archivist, graciously made available to me, with the permission of Giamatti's mother, his student records, from which the summary of his academic and extracurricular history and the assessments of his teachers are drawn.

The Andover archives contain files of *The Phillipian* and the *Andover Bulletin* (Andover's alumni magazine), from which various quotations in this chapter are taken. Giamatti's account of the return of students after Christmas is in *The Phillipian* for January 12, 1956, and his "report" to an alumni luncheon is in the *Andover Bulletin* for July 1956 (p. 32). His talk at the retirement dinner for Ted Harrison is in the Yale Library Archives. The *Bulletin* (Fall 1989, p. 25) also contains the account by Judith Sizer of her trip to meet Giamatti in New Haven.

Yale

A personal interview with Daniel Catlin, and subsequent correspondence, was particularly helpful for this chapter.

The Yale Library Archives contain Dean DeVane's 1948 report to the president ("Report of the Dean of Yale College," *Reports to the President of Yale University, 1947–48*, p. 4); and the Doob report (*Report of the President's Committee on the Freshman Year* [New Haven: Yale University Press], 1962).

Giamatti's diagnosis of the "intense skepticism" of the 1950s Yale undergraduate appears in his *History of Scroll and Key, 1942–1972* (New Haven: Kingsley Trust Association, 1978), p. 25. This volume, and Maynard Mack's history of the earlier years referred to below, were privately printed. Copies are available in the Yale Library Archives.

Alvin Kernan's vignette of the undergraduate Giamatti is in his memoir *In Plato's Cave* (New Haven: Yale University Press, 1999), p. 267.

The summary of the origins of Scroll and Key is based on Maynard Mack's *History of Scroll and Key* (New Haven: Kingsley Trust Association, 1978).

Giamatti's expression of the value of his year in Scroll and Key comes from his history cited above, p. 50.

Giamatti's class oration is printed in the 1960 *Senior Class Yearbook*, pp. 347–48, available in the Yale Library Archives.

Princeton

This chapter draws heavily on a personal interview with Robert Hollander and subsequent correspondence with him and with Alvin Kernan.

The information about Giamatti's academic career at Princeton comes from the file on him in the university's Seeley G. Mudd Manuscript Library.

Yale in the 1960s and 1970s

In this chapter, the chronology of events at Yale as reported in the *Yale Daily News* was particularly helpful. John Hersey's *Letter to the Alumni* (New York: Knopf, 1970) provided useful information and insight by a college master, especially on the May Day crisis (pp. 77–103).

Giamatti's attack on the Free Speech Movement is in an essay entitled "Sentimentality" to be found in *The University and the Public Interest* (New York: Athenaeum, 1981), pp. 39–48.

Giamatti's description of the youth movement and of the group picture of Scroll and Key seniors are from his *History* of the society, cited above, pp. 27 and 7, respectively.

Alan Bernheimer's vignette is from a letter to the author.

Deconstruction is described in a chapter entitled "Deconstructive Criticism" in Vincent B. Leitch's *American Literary Criticism from the Thirties to the Eighties* (New York: Columbia University Press, 1988). For an unsympathetic discussion of the movement, see John Ellis's *Against Deconstruction* (Princeton: Princeton University Press, 1989).

Donald Kagan's description of Giamatti's remarks to the parents of students in Ezra Stiles College is in the Giamatti memorial issue of the *Yale Weekly Bulletin and Calendar,* September 11, 1989, p. 5.

The portrait of Giamatti holding forth in the nave of Sterling Memorial Library is from an essay by student editor David Berreby entitled "Will Success Spoil A. Bartlett Giamatti?" in the *Yale Daily News Magazine,* April 1978.

Scholar

Giamatti's scholarly works discussed or referred to in this chapter are as follows:

The Earthly Paradise and the Renaissance Epic. Princeton: Princeton University Press, 1966.

Exile and Change in Renaissance Literature. New Haven: Yale University Press, 1984.

Play of Double Senses: Spenser's "Faerie Queene." Englewood Cliffs, N.J.: Prentice-Hall, 1975.

Ed. *Dante in America.* Binghamton, N.Y.: Medieval and Renaissance Texts and Studies, 1983.

Ed. (with Stewart A. Baker). *Orlando Furioso.* Trans. William Stewart Rose. New York: Bobbs-Merrill, 1968.

General ed. *Western Literature.* 3 vols. New York: Harcourt Brace Jovanovich, 1971.

Teacher

This chapter draws heavily on the reminiscences of former Yale students and others who replied to a solicitation for recollections that I placed in the *Yale Alumni Magazine.* Among those who replied are Stacy

Andersen, Diane Harmon Asher, Alan Bernheimer, Scott B. Cantor, A. James Giannini, David S. Koslow, and James Messke.

The account of Giamatti's contact with and influence on Judith Sizer is based on a personal interview with her.

President-Designate

The account of Yale's search for a new president and the selection of Giamatti draws heavily on a personal interview with Lance M. Liebman, a member of the search committee.

Allan Schoener is the author of *The Italian Americans* (New York: Macmillan, 1987).

An excellent recent portrait of Kingman Brewster and account of his career is Geoffrey Kabaservice's *The Guardians: Kingman Brewster, His Circle, and the Rise of the Liberal Establishment* (New York: Holt, 2004).

Giamatti's inaugural address is reprinted in the *Yale Alumni Magazine* for November 1978, p. 2.

Some Early Personnel Decisions

Giamatti's description of the beginning of his Yale presidency appears in *A Free and Ordered Space: The World of the University* (New York: Norton, 1988), pp. 18–19.

The account of the dismissal of Robert Brustein as dean of the Yale School of Drama is based largely on Brustein's own memoir of his years in New Haven, *Making Scenes* (New York: Random House, 1981).

The Homilies

Giamatti's talks to incoming Yale freshmen and graduating seniors were set forth as delivered in the *Yale Weekly Bulletin and Calendar* and in the *Yale Alumni Magazine*. As stated in the text, many of them, including all of those referred to in this chapter, are reprinted, sometimes in slightly revised form, in *A Free and Ordered Space*, cited above.

A. Whitney Griswold's words on the value of a liberal education in a democracy are from an essay entitled "The Creative Individual," reprinted in his *Liberal Education and the Democratic Ideal* (New Haven: Yale University Press, 1959), pp. 98–99. Clark Kerr's book is *The Uses of the University* (Cambridge: Harvard University Press, 2001).

Budget Reform

Personal interviews with Jerald Stevens and Janet Ackerman provided helpful background for this chapter.

Achieving Financial Equilibrium at Yale: A Report on the Budget (New Haven: Yale University, 1977) is available in the Yale Library Archives.

Giamatti's talk to a law school alumni lunch (copy in the Yale Library Archives) was given on October 9, 1985.

The President and New Haven

Henry Chauncey's reminiscences come from an article on Yale and New Haven in the *Yale Alumni Magazine* for December 1973, pp. 8–13, entitled "What Are We Doing Wrong? How Can We Do Better?" Chauncey and Peter Halsey provided me with further valuable observations on town-gown relations during the Brewster and Giamatti years.

Information about the Yale–New Haven Teachers Institute was made available by its longtime director James R. Vivian, who served in that capacity during Giamatti's presidency.

I am indebted to Peter Dobkin Hall's article "Is Tax Exemption Intrinsic or Contingent? The Treatment of Voluntary Associations, Nonprofit Organizations, and Religious Bodies in New Haven, Connecticut, 1750–2000," in *Property-Tax Exemption for Charities* (Washington, D.C.: Urban Institute Press, 2002), and to a personal interview with Hall, for background on Yale's property tax exemption and Giamatti's defense of it.

The Labor Crisis

My former partner at Palmer & Dodge LLP (now Edwards Angell Palmer & Dodge LLP) Jerome Weinstein, an accomplished labor lawyer, provided guidance in understanding the principles of labor law relevant to Giamatti's tactical decisions during the labor crisis.

Resignation

The circumstances of Giamatti's introduction to Fay Vincent and Vincent's role in helping him to secure a corporate position are based on a personal interview with Vincent. These events are also described in Vincent's recent book *The Last Commissioner: A Baseball Valentine* (New York: Simon and Schuster, 2002), pp. 69–72 and 77–78, respectively. The full bibliographical information on *The Ethical Investor* is John G. Simon, Charles W. Powers, and Jon P. Gunneman, *The Ethical Investor: Universities and Corporate Responsibility* (New Haven: Yale University Press, 1972).

An Appraisal

Gaddis Smith's verdict on Giamatti's presidency is included in his assessment of the first decade of Richard Levin's presidency of Yale in the *Yale Alumni Magazine,* November–December, 2003, p. 34.

Publication data for Kernan's *In Plato's Cave* are given above for the chapter entitled "Yale."

C. P. Snow's contrast between scientists and humanists is in the first of his Rede Lectures at Cambridge, collected in *The Two Cultures* (Cambridge: Cambridge University Press, 1959).

Liberal Education at Yale: The Yale College Course of Study, 1945–1978, by Daniel Catlin, Jr. (Washington, D.C.: University Press of America, 1982), summarizes Yale's curriculum requirements during the years immediately preceding Giamatti's presidency (chapters 7 and 8).

The source of the criteria for measuring the importance of a university president is Derek Bok, former president of Harvard University (1971–91), in a letter to the author.

Robert Maynard Hutchins's argument for the central place of "the great books" in a liberal education will be found in *The Great Conversation: The Substance of a Liberal Education,* vol. 1 of *Great Books of the Western World* (Chicago: Encyclopedia Brittanica, in collaboration with the University of Chicago, 1952). Publication data for Clark Kerr's study are given above for the chapter entitled "The Homilies."

The Green Fields of the Mind

The full title of Giamatti's book on baseball is *Take Time for Paradise: Americans and Their Games* (New York: Simon and Schuster, 1989).

"Baseball and the American Character," "Recall as the Series Ends, the Afternoon of the Fall," and "The Green Fields of the Mind" are reprinted in a collection of Giamatti's baseball writings entitled *A Great and Glorious Game* (Chapel Hill, N.C.: Algonquin, 1998).

National League President and Commissioner of Baseball

Tim Wiles at the Baseball Hall of Fame archive was helpful in a variety of ways in facilitating access to materials in the archive's collections for this chapter and the next.

Giamatti's decision in the Kevin Gross case and his essay on Tom Seaver appear in *A Great and Glorious Game,* cited in the notes to the preceding chapter.

The account of Giamatti's initiative in creating an enlarged library and archive at the Baseball Hall of Fame is based on correspondence and a telephone interview with Tom Heitz, then the librarian.

Roger Angell's "Celebration" first appeared in *The New Yorker* for August 20, 1988, and his "The Web of the Game" first appeared in the same magazine for July 20, 1981. Both are reprinted in Angell's *Once More Around the Park: A Baseball Reader* (New York: Ballantine, 1991).

Vincent describes his role in negotiating Giamatti's contract as commissioner in *The Last Commissioner* (pp. 83–84), cited above in the notes to the chapter entitled "Resignation."

The Pete Rose Affair

The principal sources for the Rose affair were the Dowd report, cited below, and *Collision at Home Plate,* by James Reston, Jr., cited above, especially chapters 9 through 11.

A valuable source for this chapter and the next was the section entitled "Bart and Rose" (pp. 103–36) in Fay Vincent's *The Last Commissioner.*

The standard source for the events of the Black Sox scandal and the role of Landis is Eliot Asinof's *Eight Men Out* (New York: Holt, 1963). See also J. G. Taylor Spink's *Judge Landis and 25 Years of Baseball* (New York: Cromwell, 1947), especially chapters 8 through 11.

The Dowd report ("In the Matter of Peter Edward Rose, Manager, Cincinnati Reds Baseball Club: Report to the Commissioner, May 9, 1989") is available, with exhibits, in the A. Bartlett Giamatti Research Center at the Baseball Hall of Fame.

Coda

A transcript of the proceedings at Yale's memorial service for Giamatti is in the Yale Library Archives.

The quoted reminiscences of Linda Lorimer and Ellen Scantlebury appear in the Giamatti memorial issue of the *Yale Weekly Bulletin and Calendar,* September 11, 1989. Fay Vincent's recollection and tribute are taken from *The Last Commissioner,* pp. 69 and 134.

Interviews

The people named below spoke to me in person or by telephone or email about Giamatti. I am indebted to them for their contributions, great and small.

Janet Ackerman	Alvin Kernan
Sidney Altman	Howard Lamar
John Morton Blum	Lance Liebman
Marie Boroff	Linda Lorimer
Peter Brooke	Maynard Mack
Guido Calabresi	Louis Martz
Daniel Catlin	William Mazeine
Henry Chauncey, Jr.	Philip Paolello
Frank Converse	Daniel Quint
Thomas Crosby	Leon Rosenberg
Elria Ewing	Haj Ross
Dino Giamatti	Maxine Singer
Peggy Giamatti	Judith Sizer
Russel Goddard	Gaddis Smith
Abraham Goldstein	Jerald Stevens
Stephen Gurney	Charles Taylor
Peter Dobkin Hall	Steven Umin
Peter Halsey	Fay Vincent
Thomas Heitz	Jerome Weinstein
Terry Holcombe	Tim Wiles
Robert Hollander	John Wilkinson
Donald Kagan	

Index